First Church

**Memorial of the one hundredth anniversary of the**

**organization of the First Church**

First Church

**Memorial of the one hundredth anniversary of the organization of the First Church**

ISBN/EAN: 9783337260163

Printed in Europe, USA, Canada, Australia, Japan

Cover: Foto ©Lupo / pixelio.de

More available books at **www.hansebooks.com**

# Memorial

OF THE

# One Hundredth Anniversary

OF THE

# Organization Of The First Church,

AND

# Ordination of The First Settled Town Minister

OF

# Wakefield, N. H.

WAKEFIELD:
PRINTED FOR THE PARISH.
1886.

Printed by GEO. S. DORR at the PIONEER Office,

WOLFBORO' JUNCTION, (WAKEFIELD) N. H.

# THE MEMORIAL OCCASION.

At a parish meeting held in June, some three months before the event, it was voted to celebrate on Tuesday the twenty-second day of September next, the One Hundredth Anniversary of the Organization of the First Church and of the Ordination of the First Settled Town Minister, and a committee was appointed from the church and congregation to make arrangements.

Dea. Satchell Weeks, Dea. George H. Gage, George F. Piper, grandson of the first minister, secretary, Rev. Albert H. Thompson, corresponding secretary; also Mrs. Mary A. Yeaton, Mrs. Mary P. Paul, Mrs. Olive E. Brown. Later, it being also a town matter, the committee was enlarged to embrace many others belonging to the early families of Wakefield, including the grand-daughter of the first deacon, Miss Lucy M. Sawyer, and Miss Harriette Dow, the grand-daughter of the third deacon, Richard Dow. The committee made necessary arrangements, inviting former pastors living, who reported in person or by letter, all living ministers who have gone out of this church, ministers of the several denominations in town with other friends of Wakefield stock.

The day was a day of beauty, and five hundred gathered to pay tribute to the character of their ancestors and to praise the God of their fathers. The service at the Meeting-house, and at the Town House, where a bountiful repast was served, was evidently satisfactory to all. The house of worship was plain, with but little decoration, and the spirit of the fathers was prevalent. The Service of Song was participated in by the Congregational and Episcopal choirs and other singers. The program, as printed on following pages, was essentially carried out, Hon. John W. Sanborn presiding. Rev. George O. Jenness, not being able to be present, the Invocation was given by Rev. Gardner S. Butler, pastor of the Congregational church at Union Village, in Wakefield, formerly a part of this parish. Rev. William Lloyd Himes, the Rector of the Church of St. John the Baptist, also in Wakefield, led the Responsive Reading of the Psalms 122 and 148 : 1-16, the people giving the responses heartily. After the hymn following the Historical Address, Hon. Seth Low, the Mayor of Brooklyn, the great grandson of Richard Dow, one of the pioneers of the church, gave a cordial and capable address.

In the afternoon the services were in charge of Pastor Thompson, who led in the Responsive Reading of 23d Psalm and in prayer. The addresses were informal and not preserved for publication, but their equivalents are placed upon the following pages for our satisfaction and for their's who shall come after us.                    A. H. T.

Wakefield, Dec. 1, 1885.

# The One Hundredth Anniversary

OF THE

## Organization Of The First Church,

IN

## Wakefield, N. H.

AND OF THE

## Ordination of The First Settled Minister

BY A COUNCIL CALLED BY THE TOWN.

## SEPTEMBER 22, 1785.

*The Minister was* - - - - *ASA PIPER.*

**The Members of the Church were**
SAMUEL HAINES, SIMEON DEARBORN, AVERY HALL, MAYHEW CLARK, RICHARD DOW,
with the wives of the last four.

The Moderator of the Town Meeting — *1785* — SIMEON DEARBORN.

The President of the Day        —*1885*— JOHN W. SANBORN.

Corresponding Secretary, · · · · · ALBERT H. THOMPSON.
Wakefield, September 22, 1885.

# Order of Exercises.

**9.30 A. M.**

A Service of Songs of Olden Time.      Freeman D. Pike, Precentor.

**10.00 A. M**

Address of Welcome by                      Hon. John W. Sanborn.

Response by                        Hon. Joshua G. Hall, of Dover.

Invocation,            Rev. G. O. Jenness, Pastor, 1875-80.

Responsive Psalm Reading—122.

Hymn, "Coronation"

Prayer,            Rev. Sumner Clark, Pastor, 1872-75.

Original Hymn,            Rev. D. D. Tappan, Pastor, 1865-70.

Tune.—Missionary Chant.

God of the Centuries! Thy truth
  Has thro' the ages kept its way,
And still maintains a vigorous youth,
  With ever widening. lustrous sway.

So, too, thy church, her Guide in view,
  From times remote has kept her course.
Dispensing good like early dew,
  Of human weal a faithless source.

Thanks be to him whose precious blood
  Redeemed the church from sin and woe;
Who will present all pure to God,
  Those that confess him here below.

This hundredth year of her birthday,
  This little flock thy care would own,
And grateful homage here would pay,
  As thus we bow before the throne.

Though, one by one. our numbers cease
  For higher ministries above.
The Savior ne'er withdraws his peace.
  His gracious guardianship and love.

Whate'er mutations time may bring,
  What foes, what perils we may meet,
The joy remains that Christ, our King,
  Will be our friend in every state.

**10.45 A. M.**

Historical Address,            Rev. A. H. Thompson, Pastor. 1880-

Hymn, "I love thy Church, O God."

Poem,            Miss Harriet N. Hobbs.

Doxology, "Praise God from whom all blessings flow."

**12.30 P. M.**

Dinner at the Town Hall.

**2.00 P. M.**

Informal addresses from past Pastors, Ministers of the town, and Letters, with Addresses from Hon. J. G. Hall, Hon. Seth Low, Hon. J. W. Sanborn, and other friends.

"Auld Lang Syne" will be sung at the close.

# ADDRESS OF WELCOME.

BY HON. JOHN W. SANBORN.

LADIES AND GENTLEMEN:

We have met here to-day on a very interesting occasion, to celebrate the one hundredth anniversary of the organization of the first Congregational Church in Wakefield; and to me has been assigned the pleasant duty of presiding at this meeting. I take it for granted that whatever our individual opinions upon religious questions, or religious subjects, may be, we are all agreed on one point, and that is, religious organizations are necessary for the good order and well-being of society in every community; and that we all feel interested in the success of every properly organized and well conducted religious society, and therefore feel interested in the success of this society. One hundred years ago to-day this Church was organized. It was not the Church alone, that was interested on that occasion, but the whole people of the town were also interested; they had, in their corporate capacity, held meetings and elected committees at various times, to employ a Minister of the Gospel, and after corresponding with several candidates, they made arrangements with Rev. Asa Piper to come here and settle. Accordingly, on the 22d day of September, 1785, he was ordained by a Council called by the town, for that purpose, as the town's Minister; they having agreed to pay him a fixed salary; on the same day this Church was organized, and he installed as its pastor. He was thus called upon to perform the duties of a dual office—

minister of the town, and pastor of the church; these duties
he ably and faithfully performed for twenty-five long years,
when, for certain considerations, he "absolved" the town
from all liability on the original contract, but remained pastor of the church until the infirmities of age compelled him
to resign. He was a learned man, a wise counsellor, and
an able teacher; his impress was firmly fixed upon our people, and to him we are, in a great degree, indebted for our
prosperity. The church organization has been kept intact
to the present time, and under its influences, and other good
influences, the town has raised a people that for ability and
integrity has compared favorably with any town in the
State. Many of the sons and daughters of Wakefield have
left their birthplace to become citizens of other towns and
other states, have won almost enviable reputations there,
have held important positions with honor to themselves and
credit to their native town, and while those of us who have
remained here have endeavored to keep up the standard long
ago established, so far as we have been able, we have also
watched them with a parent's care, and rejoiced in their success, and are always ready to bid them welcome to our home.
Some of them are here to-day, and to them let me say, I bid
you welcome, yea, a thrice hearty welcome. And now, in
behalf of the committee of arrangements, and in behalf of
this church and society, I bid all present, whether residents
or non-residents, native or foreign born, a hearty welcome,
and most cordially invite you to join in commemorating the
event we have met to celebrate, and I trust, for the purposes
of this celebration, we shall all feel we are members of one
society and one people.

The President then introduced Hon. Joshua G. Hall, as
one of Wakefield's honored sons, who spoke as follows:

MR. PRESIDENT:

I am asked on behalf of the returning Sons and
Daughters of this now ancient Parish and Town to express
their appreciation of your kindly welcome to the old home.
We are met at the century mile stone of this church. Those

of us who from time to time have gone out from the Town
and made homes elsewhere and those who have steadfastly
adhered to the paternal acres and maintained the civiliza-
tion and religion planted here by our Fathers meet together
to show our respect and veneration for the first settlers of
this hamlet and testify our deep appreciation of their life
work here in the cause of civil order and Christianity, and
I assure you that those of us who return here from abroad
to take part in this joyous occasion reverence the Fathers
as deeply and appreciate as fully the grand work of the
first generations as do you who have always made your
home within the limits of Wakefield. You could not have
done less if you would be dutiful and reverent children than
call us wanderers in to this feast of commemoration that
we may together recount the sayings and doings of a revered ancestry and rehabilitate so far as we may by tradition
and reminiscence the vanished forms of the Pastor and people of a hundred years ago.

It is said that comparisons are odious, and we must admit that the American mind is given to boasting, but I
think we have a right to say, and that no one will take of-
fence at the saying, that this church and town at their start
were made up of more than common good stock. I think
if we were to take a list of the early settlers of this town
both men and women and recount the life of each so far as
it has come down to us, pretty full and quite complete in
many cases, though scanty in others, it would appear that
the older settlements in the lower part of the state—for our
Fathers came generally from Rockingham County and the
southerly part of Strafford—furnished for the emigration
hither of the flower of their youth and of the strongest and
best of their men and women of middle life. Of the settlers who came here early a very large proportion came from
families of prominence and high standing in the older towns of
the province. Generally they were well abreast of the times
in matters of education and no Town in this vicinity could
boast among its citizens so many men of liberal culture as

Wakefield in its early days. The men of a century ago who founded this Town and this church, who welcomed the first Pastor and here listened to his ministrations were men of force and strong power of brain. They wrought well for the church and the state and the impression made by their earnest lives is I fancy still a power for good to us. And while the home hive has well maintained its place in the state considering the changes in the currents of business and the shifting of popular centres, the swarms that have gone out from time to time have done their part in shaping and moulding public sentiment about them. But it is not my province on this occasion to recount the history of the hundred years past. That is to be treated of in formal discourse by another. The occasion is a notable one. We meet where the centuries divide. We come to gather glimpses of the past and recount the virtues of the Fathers and Mothers who struggled and wrought as best they might for their posterity and have passed from sight. We come to take counsel of their shining example and express our devotion to the perpetuity of the three institutions that were uppermost in their minds—The Church, The School, The Town. The same bending Heavens are above us and the same green earth is at our feet that Minister and People looked out on a hundred years ago, but changed, changed as the skill, endurance, persistence and Christian faith of a hundred years of New England life only, can change the face of the earth. May the memories that come to us be pleasant and may we rejoice that we see this day of commemoration.

Following the remarks of Mr. Hall came Devotional Exercises as indicated by the program, with slight variations as to those taking part, mentioned elsewhere, after which the President introduced the Rev. A. H. Thompson as the Historian of the day, who gave the following:

# HISTORICAL ADDRESS.

REV. ALBERT H. THOMPSON.

OLD FRIENDS AND NEW FRIENDS OF ANCIENT WAKEFIELD AND MODERN WAKEFIELD:

The mantle of your historian for this day might have fallen on more worthy shoulders—on some son of Wakefield, though he might blush to praise his ancestors—yet I cheerfully submit, as one proud to speak as an adopted son of these adopted ancestors. I would weave, if I could, a romance of beauty to charm you, or better, I would thrill you, not with dry and dull statistics, but with the story of their virtues and valiant deeds. But history is scant and I must give you the prose of the records.

There is an old adage, "Great oaks from little acorns grow." But our song to-day is not of the giant oak, but of the tiny acorn, planted in the soil of good old Wakefield one hundred years ago. And, because the church has reached that age, we revere the memory of the Infant church brought into being September the twenty-second, 1785. Five were the men and four the women—wives, too, of the four men, and the fifth wife came in the next year. Beautiful is this picture of these Homes consecrated to God by the united love to God of both the partners.

Could any church have a better start? Could a community be blessed more richly than in a church made up of consecrated homes? Not merely a body, as usual, of individual believers, this was stronger—a union of Christian homes, a combination of families for the worship and service of God. The patriarch Abram with his family may have been at one time the church of God on earth. If only one godly family was in a community, that would be the church. These husbands and wives may not have been the only Christians in Wakefield on that clear September morn, 1785, but they are the heroes of our song:—Samuel Haines,

Avery Hall, Abigail Hall, Richard Dow, Mary Dow, Simeon Dearborn, Martha Dearborn, Mayhew Clark, Mary Clark. Descendants they have, who may well praise the God of their fathers who gave them such an ancestry, not descended from royal blood, but princes and princesses in in the everlasting Kingdom.

What led to the organization of this church at this time? We answer,—they tell us in part, and we know two facts that would be likely to affect their action. The war of the Revolution had ended four years before, its thunders had died away, and the people were settling down to the labors and arts of peace, to build up the young nation whose liberty they had purchased on the bloody battle field. And to this end the Christian church would add its great influence. Again, the town for several years had cared for its own religious welfare instead of allowing private individuals so to do, as now, and voted each year to have preaching four, six or eight weeks by some minister designated by the town, with attempts at permanent settlement in 1779-80-82. Now, increased in population and resources, and possibly, more awake to the religious need, the people, in town meeting assembled, proposed to have a minister the year round, just as much as a selectman or pound keeper, and to keep alive and awake the religious spirit, as well as to keep the roads and bridges in good condition that society may have a safe journey.

It is this determined effort to keep alive the worship and service of God that we seek to commemorate. Not the establishing and success of a particular rival branch of God's church, outstripping all other branches in its growth, though we rejoice that God has set the seal of his approval thereon by making that infant of hours the Centenarian of to-day. It was not the effort of a few sectarians to establish their sect, nor really of Christians to establish Christianity. It was the town, made up, as now, of saints and sinners, aiming to care for its spiritual as well as material welfare; and very likely they were shrewd enough to see that the material prosperity would be enhanced by the spiritual.

Eighteen years before, the winter of 1767, the first family wintered in town, or two families by the name of Gilman, father and son. In 1769 the number had increased to eleven. The next year nineteen more made thirty. In 1784, our date, three times thirty. In 1800, five times thirty. The first death, that of an infant child. So reads the diary of the first minister. The first child who lived, probably, Dorothy Quimby, born June 30, 1768, who married Nathaniel Willey of Brookfield. Also, "1771, a meeting house was raised, and the outside nearly finished when the commencement of the Revolution in 1775 interupted it." This was the first and only town meeting house, erected when the number of inhabitants was not large, who yet wanted a place in which to meet for political and religious purposes, and was finished years afterward. In 1820 succeeded by the new meeting house, so called, at Wakefield Corner, which latter was used for religious purposes below and educational above, while the Town House for perhaps fifty years has been used for strictly secular town business.

But going back to 1774. In that year the town ceased to be called East-town and was incorporated as Wakefield, in honor of whom I cannot say, but in the reign of "George the Third, by the grace of God of Great Britain, France and Ireland King, Defender of the Faith", etc., John Wentworth, Esq., Governor and Commander-in-Chief of our Province, and of our Council—"all white pine trees reserved forever for the use of our royal navy"—and Capt. David Copp authorized to call the first town meeting within seventy days from date, August 30, 1774. Of that meeting we have no record at hand. The earliest accessible record is in that eventful year of Concord and Lexington, when the colonies began the struggle to free themselves from the yoke of the "tyrant". Yet our early settlers did not forget to pray and to worship. For in May, 1775, the town met (1) "To see if the town will vote to have any preaching this summer, and if any, what method they will take to hire it. (2) To see what method the town will take with those men that inlisted as minit-men. (3) To hear the request of William Blaisdell relative to exchanging more or all of the school lot with said Blaisdell. Signed, Simeon Dearborn, Noah Kimball, Joseph Malcham, selectmen." So they were probably chosen at the first meeting. At the second town meeting, July 17, it was voted "that there be preaching;" "that there be eight Sabbaths preaching here at the expense of the town unless the proprietors are bound by charter to supply this. Voted that Mr. Henshaw be the man. Voted that Mr. Jonathan Gilman, Simeon Dearborn, Esq., and Mr. John Horn be a committee to apply to Mr. Henshaw, or some other suitable person, if he cannot be had." The names of the proprietors are unknown but by few. Each year the military and religious concerns occupied the mind of the citizens of Wakefield as the chief concerns—to supply the army with soldiers and the town with preaching. These are the names of preachers mentioned: 1775, Henshaw; 1776, Chickering or Henshaw and Hall, perhaps Avery Hall who had moved in from Rochester where he was pastor for nine years up to 1775; 1777, Mr. Porter, very likely later the distinguished Dr. Nathaniel Porter, born in Topsfield, Mass., in 1745, graduate of Harvard college in 1768, ordained at New Durham to the Christian ministry, and after serving the church at Conway, of which he was ordained pastor some ten weeks after its organization in 1778, Aug. 18, for fifty years, he died in 1836, at the great age of 91; of whom it is said, "He endured great privations here; he worked by day and wrote his sermons by the light of pitch-wood at night." 1778, Rev. Mr. Dutch and Cummings; 1779, Mr. Henshaw again, and Mr. Dutch was called to settle; 1780, Rev. Josiah Badcock, 60 voted for his settlement, 15 against; 1781, Rev. Mr. Kendall; 1782-83, Rev. Moses Sweat, who seems to have got a hold of the affections of many, and a mild contest took place, according to the record, whether or not he should be the permanent supply. Once the town voted to have no Sweat that year. The next they voted yes, but he declined. The reason given by tradition is not given by the uninspired Town Clerk, and I will not give it, only advise all ministers to be careful in their horse trades. He seems to have had a reputation more as a great Greek and Hebrew scholar to whom great scholars looked as an authority. His home, as pastor for many years, was in Sanford, Me., where he died in 1824 at the age of three score and ten. In the year 1782 the earnest desire for constant religious worship showed itself in the call for all the legal voters to meet at the Meeting House "for the purpose of consulting upon our religious affairs, and to come into and prosecute such measures as the Town shall think fit when met, in order to have the Gospel preached among us. The matter of Religion, with the means appointed for the promoting of it, are so important that we shall be acquitted of Blame, yea, commended for calling the Town together at this busy time, and desiring all concerned to attend as above mentioned. Avery Hall, John Wingate, Mayhew Clark." At the notified meeting Aug. 26, Capt. David Copp, moderator, it was voted to adjourn one week. Then it was voted "to keep Thursday, 12th day of instant September, as a Day of Fasting and Prayer for Direction in the calling and settling of a minister." "Voted also to invite the Rev. Messrs. James Pike, Jeremy Belknap, Joseph Haven, Isaac Hasey, Nehemiah Ordway, to assist and advise on that occasion." This was a council called not by a church but by the town, Esq. Dearborn, Capt. D. Copp and Avery Hall to be a committee to write to these ministers. No permanent minister was advised, but Esq. Dearborn, Capt. Copp, Mr. Nathaniel Balch, Mr. Richard Dow and Mr. Avery Hall were chosen to hire for a term not exceeding two months. Though they did not get what they proposed, this record shows the spirit of our ancestors anxious for a "meeting". In 1782 so earnest were they to secure permanent public worship that a Town meeting was called and a Fast Day appointed, as we have seen. This shows the spirit of our ancestors.

Their desires were at last gratified in 1784. In the spring of that year it was voted to have eight Sabbaths preaching, Capt. Copp, Ensign Clark and Major Palmer, a committee "to apply to some suitable person to preach with us on probation 4 Sabbaths at first." In the August meeting, Lieut. Jonathan Gilman, moderator, "voted to hire eight Sabbaths preaching in Addition to what was voted last spring. Simeon Dearborn, Esq., Avery Hall and Mr. Richard Dow to be a new committee to hire a candidate on Probation at Discretion, and meeting dissolved." November, the town met and voted to give a call to the man selected by this committee [at Cambridge], and he accepted. This ended the yearly supply. I have given the names of the successive ministers who served the town only a few weeks, but long enough to show their excellence and the taste of the people. And judging by the later renown of Sweat and Porter, that, even in their younger days at Wakefield they must have shown some of that power of mind, we may judge that all these early town ministers of Wakefield were fully up to the average of those days. Their service was limited, and we pass them by with a brief notice, which they surely deserve. They were the Forerunners of the Settled Minister.

A new era dawns upon the town, when, in 1784, there appears in Wakefield a young minister, twenty-seven years old, of staunch English stock, whose great grandfather came from Dartmouth, in England, in the time of the Revolution which resulted in the dethronement of the King Charles I, who, with the ruling passion strong in death, declaring that the *people had no right to any part in the government*, calmly placed his head upon the block, was beheaded, and England was without a King, and parliament governed England and established a republic under the title of the commonwealth, which lasted eleven years. During this period, the ancestor came to America and settled in Ipswich, Mass. The struggle in the land of his birth, without doubt, had its impress on his character, and that of his descendants. The great grandfather witnessed the revolution in England; the great grandson was a young man of eighteen, when the guns of Lexington and Concord, within a few miles of his home at Acton, sounded the beginning of the Revolution, which should result in the independence of the colonies. Those were stirring times, as 125 years before in the mother country. So, I say of this young minister who appeared in Wakefield in 1784,—of staunch English stock, not a soldier of the Revolution, but a thorough patriot, as shown by his eloquent address on the death of Washington, and his early home would make him so;—a good scholar and priest of the Most High God. Nine and forty years he lived not far from the beautiful lake, until on the 17th day of May, 1835, he died very suddenly, much lamented by the church and the citizens of the town generally,—Rev. Asa Piper, the first pastor of this church, the first and only settled Town minister. He stands at the head of the line in time and talent. His successors must have mention, though it be brief. In 1828, Rev. Samuel Nichols was ordained as colleague pastor, serving as such until 1833, when he was dismissed by council. He was a graduate of Bangor Theological Seminary, 1826, a native of South Reading, Mass., where he died in 1844, in the forty-sixth year of his age. As a preacher, he may not have ranked high for brilliancy, but the comparatively large number of additions in his short ministry, of over forty to the membership of nine at his arrival, speaks well of the spiritual condition of the society. Six weeks after our first minister was laid away in his peaceful grave, but a few steps from the sacred house where was his throne, there came another minister, not quite forty years of age,— Nathaniel Barker, and he lived among you, lo, these many years, that life of a holy man, until, scarce two years since, he was called away, at four score and seven, to the Reward of the Faithful. He also was a college graduate, sharing with Dartmouth the honor of one of her sons in 1822. Revolutionary blood and the martyr spirit was in his veins. His father, Samuel Barker, a soldier of the Revolution, of heroic mould. His mother, Betsy Rogers, the daughter of Major Rogers of royal descent, tracing back his ancestry to the fires of Smithfield and to John Rogers the martyr. Born and bred in a Christian household, educated for the gospel ministry, a graduate of Andover, 1825, ordained at Mendon, Mass. soon after, where he served a few years, with a heart bound up in the cause of the Redeemer, he was led by Providence to Wakefield, in New Hampshire, just after the departure to the better land of the aged first pastor, who, like himself, had come to this same Wakefield half a century before. He once told me, speaking of the liquor traffic, then quite brisk, "I thought, if I did my duty, I shouldn't stay long." But the Lord gave him nearly fifty years longer. as the village pastor and upright citizen, and never did his voice or heart shut up to the blight of that curse, or any other which sin has brought into the world. He now sleeps in the burial place on the brow of the hill, revered in the memory of all.

His successors were, Marvin Leffingwell, of Methodist training, who did a faithful work, of four years, before 1860. Joseph B. Tufts, from 1861 to 1864, during which period several were added to the church. These are all dead. From November 19, 1865, to April 1, 1871, the now venerable, still vivacious and exact, Daniel Dana Tappan, labored in season and out of season, for the upbuilding of Zion, and the full harvest is not yet. From his pen, gifted even down to four score and seven years of age, is the grand hymn we have just sung, which lacks only his presence and voice,

"God of the Centuries! thy truth
Has through the ages held its way."

During his time of service, five days before Christmas, in the year 1867, the bell, weighing 819 pounds, and costing $388.73, of which $100 was contributed by friends away, was joined to the church, the first church bell in town, to call with its silver tones the people to the house of God; and I am glad that so many have heard and answered, and also sorry that so many have not heard nor answered. Rev. Alvan Tobey served the church for a short time, in 1871, I think. Rev. Sumner Clark, our near neighbor and firm friend, present with us to-day, with agreeable memories of the three years, from May, 1872, that he spent with his Wakefield parish, since which time he has passed the years of his retirement, but not of slothfulness, in our sister town of Wolfeboro', still holding in your hearts a large place. The five years before 1880, were marked by a signal display of the grace of God, especially among the young, in the ministry of Rev. Geo. O. Jenness, who, only two or three Sabbaths since, gave from this desk the message to his old congregation, as in days gone by, and to-day, regretting his inability to be present, as do we, he sends greeting and his heartiest well wishes. During the eighties, the feeble light of your historian has been shed, and it is to him a pleasure and a pride to be serving in this Centennial year, this ancient church, and to recount with you the deeds of your pious ancestors. Leaving the latter fifty or seventy-five years, with very limited notices of the ministers, we shall find abundant food for reflection in the first quarter of a century, the time when Asa Piper was the Town's minister.

You have already noticed that the earlier preachers were educated men, who believed in studying the Bible in the languages in which it was written, the Hebrew and Greek. Without sacrificing the religious nature, they aimed to develop the mind. They were the patrons of learning, and, without doubt, had something to do in forming that literary taste which has prevailed in Wakefield, and sent many a young man to college, to hold in everlasting remembrance the names of Dartmouth, of Harvard, of Yale and Bowdoin. These preachers were loyal citizens, not monks seeking retirement from the world in cloisters and caves. They were ever fearless in the discharge of what conscience told them was duty. But I would not exalt the clergy at the expense of other citizens, and we may pay to them the well deserved tribute of praise, that they considered the sanctuary a blessing to the community, and sought to support its services with their purse and presence. I should like now to see them gathered on the Lord's day in the old meeting house, with its square, high-backed pews or pens, its three galleries, its huge sounding board, over the stalwart form of the minister dressed in knee breeches, ancient coat, powdered hair, preaching to our ancestors that good old sermon ninety-nine years ago, which I gave last Sabbath, on the reverence due to the house of God. And they came from near and from far, on horse-back and on ox sleds, and barefooted to save their shoes when they should enter the sacred place. Those were the days when sacrifices were known.

Eight weeks of preaching seems to us small, but it cleared the law, and eight weeks preaching then might be as good as three times that now. But that didn't satisfy them. After they got the Revolution off their hands, and even before that time attempting it, we find them engaging a minister by the year, and each man, by vote of the town, was taxed for that object; and I am not going to say, even at this enlightened day, that it was unjust taxation. The prevailing sentiment was that Public Religious Worship was needed for the welfare of the town, as much as schools and bridges, and the town should furnish one as well as the other. So public worship would be maintained, as it ought to be, even if the town take it in hand, whereas, if left to a few, it would sink, and the town suffer. Then, it could be safely left only with the town. Now, we think it safe to leave it with anybody but the town. The church and state are separated. Possibly the separation of education from the state might give more of that boasted liberty to the individual. We need not argue for or against the old method. Perhaps we have outgrown it. We know that, according to custom, the town of Wakefield did, for the first ten years, support preaching, and then called to a permanent settlement, a minister who accepted, the Rev. Asa Piper, who had already preached nineteen Sabbaths. This call was given in November, 1784, through a committee of seven, S. Dearborn, N. Balch, A. Hall, Lt. Jona. Gilman, Capt. J. Gilman, Maj. Jona. Palmer and Ensign Mayhew Clark. The terms of settlement, or the Proposals, were :—Mr. Piper was to receive,

"In addition to the rights sequestered to the use of the Ministry in the Town, one Hundred Pounds lawful money towards building him a house, to be paid in Labor and Materials for building, common labor at 3s per day, the man finding himself; Pine Boards at 4 Dols. per 1000 ft.; Shingle at 9s per 1000, Clapboards, rough, at 4 dollars per 1000, each of said articles to be delivered on the spot, and in any other articles that may be wanted at cash price, and also lay out one hundred Days' work in Fencing and clearing the Minister's Lot. That the town will give said Mr. Piper as an annual salary, Seventy-five pounds, lawful Money, forty pounds of said sum to be paid in Money, the other thirty-five in produce of the country,—twelve pounds in Indian corn at 3s per bushel, six pounds in Rie at 4s per bushel, five pounds in Beef at 2 1-2d per lb., twelve pounds in pork at 5 pence per lb It is to be understood, that for the two first years, they will give only sixty pounds annually as salary, and after that adding to the sixty pounds yearly five pounds, until it amount to seventy-five pounds, his stated annual salary."

Also voted to give the upper part of the town, above Ensign Mayhew Clark's, a proportional part of the preaching. The proposals were modified in June, so that one-half of the 100£ settlement shall be paid the first year, the other half the next. "The work shall be done the coming fall. The Rie shall be at 3s 9d per bushel ; Money part to be paid quarterly." The minister wanted less pork and more corn, so the twelve pounds in pork was changed to the same value in Indian corn. To this call, borne by S. Dearborn, Esq., Capt. David Copp and Avery Hall, Mr. Piper made the following answer in the affirmative :

WAKEFIELD, June 20, 1785.

FRIENDS AND BRETHREN: It is sometime since I received an invitation to settle with you in the gospel ministry—a work that is not to be undertaken without a solemn pause and mature deliberation upon the reasons operating for or against compliance. Notwithstanding the great distance from my particular friends, which is a circumstance disagreeable both to them and to me, and other objections,—so remote from my brethren in the ministry, whose society and kind offices would be a source of satisfaction and edification, and likewise the difficult and laborious duty of the ministerial office to which I feel myself so unequal and unworthy of. Yet, as there appears so great a degree of unanimity (as far as I have obtained information) among the people, and as you have so far complied with what was proposed as an amendment to the former conditions; after consulting with those whose advice I esteemed; and seeking direction from the great Head of the church, with whom is the residue of the spirit, who is able to supply every weakness and deficiency, and qualify the most unworthy for his service, and on whose blessing success depends, I have finally thought it my duty not to refuse your request, and do accordingly accept your invitation. Relying, however, if a union should take place, on your Christianity and benevolence that, should the future prosperity of the Town admit of it, you will make me such further allowance as shall be necessary. And I shall expect, likewise, the privilege of absence a number of Sabbaths yearly in order to visit my friends and acquaintances to the westward.                                 ASA PIPER.

"Friends and brethren" he calls the citizens of the town. But the friends thought another step needed to secure a permanent minister, and we have what now would be a strange sight, a council called by the town for the ordination of a religious teacher, and at the same time, the "brethren" and their wives were embodied into a church by the Town's council. The town leads; the church follows. Now, in calling a minister, the church leads.

So our centennial is of the church, and of the ordination of the Town Minister, and we are to acknowledge, both as a town and as a church, as friends and as brethren, what our ancestors did for the religious help of the town.

The church was broad in its foundation, with a very limited creed, and a generous covenant: "We profess a serious and full belief that the Scriptures of the Old and New Testaments are given by inspiration; that they teach us the the doctrine of man's apostacy from God, and the only means of recovery is by faith in Jesus Christ, as the only Savior of lost sinners." A little later, in some towns, the first church organized had no creed—simply a covenant to join together Christians of different names. This short confession of Faith was later, and in 1828, at the time of set-

tling the colleague, enlarged and arranged in eight articles.
The covenant seemed to be the main thing on which they
depended for mutual help, though, of course, the covenant
was based on the kinship of belief and practice, and the object of upbuilding the kingdom of grace.   It had an "exception" as a relic of the "half-way covenant," which allowed
people to be church members and yet not partake of the
Lord's supper.   In the very early days of the Massachusetts colony, only church members could hold office in a
town ; and as men in those days were willing to hold office
if thrust upon them, they were willing to be church members.   That rule now might increase the number of men in
our churches.   One excellent woman, without doubt, was
taken into the church on "exception" in 1787, her conscience
forbidding her to partake of the Lord's Supper, and for
over forty years she was deprived of that privilege.   The
Articles of Faith have been amended, in 1828, and again in
1867.   This church now is supposed to be in general accord
with other churches of the Congregational name, but at the
outset that name is not used.   Neither is it called the first
church of Christ, though they make a solemn surrender of
themselves to the Deity in Trinity, and "regard it our in-
cumbent duty in our present situation to form ourselves into a church for fellowship and communion."   But it was the
First church of Wakefield, and I am glad that it was not
the last one, but other Christian bands, bearing different
names, have had the name of Christ written on their hearts,
and have done a good work, and their representatives are
with us.   Thus embodied, they are a simple band of humble believers, with the added beauty and power of a union
of families, who might have left their religion in their old
homes, and used the spare time in building up solely the material interests of the town.   But they were either addicted
to religious habits, or were wise enough to foresee that this
action of theirs to maintain religious worship might secure
a blessing that would enrich the town for generations to
come.   So they became a band of Christians, organized

and seconding the praiseworthy effort of the town to secure public worship and a stated ministry, that should be at once sound in the faith and learned. This was found, both by the town and church, in Asa Piper as religious Teacher and their Pastor. The moderator of the special town meeting which called him was Simeon Dearborn. The moderator of the new church meeting was Avery Hall, and the voted call was unanimous, and this was the answer given that very day, before his ordination, Wakefield, Sept. 22, 1785 :

"I now declare my acceptance of the call given me this day by the church of Christ in this place to be their pastor.   ASA PIPER.

The town had already called him to be their minister, and he had accepted three months before. The town led. The church followed. And when the town totally ceased, as it had been gradually yielding its right, to lead, at the passage of the Toleration Act about 1819,—and virtually before, as we shall see, the church remained as the organized spiritual body, competent to call and settle a minister, and the First Congregational SOCIETY was chartered by the Legislature in 1815, which embraced Joseph Wiggin, Richard Dow, Luther Dearborn, William Sawyer, Joshua G. Hall, John Kimball, Elisha Sanborn.

The organizing of the church that day tempers for us the secular appearance of the meeting. The state was not the church, but it protected it, and regarded itself bound to furnish and sustain, as well as to protect, public worship. But I dwell too long. This justifies us in regarding this as something more than a church celebration, and in honoring the action of those in town who believed that a town without religion is worse than a church and state working together —or the state as the church—for the welfare of the community.

The members of the ordaining council were ministers Hasey of Lebanon, Me., Haven of Rochester, Adams of Acton, Mass., the early home of the young minister, Newhall of Stowe, Mass., Ripley of Concord, Mass., the last three from good old Revolutionary ground. The diary of Parson Hasey gives this condensed report: "September 22, 1785. Chiefly clear; rode to ordination at Wakefield. Newhall prayed; Adams preached; Hasey prayed and charge; Haven right hand; Ripley last prayer. Sept. 23, rode home A. M., Mr. Spring with me." Thus, on the 22d day of September, Asa Piper saw this church organized, received its call and accepted it, was ordained, and married his first couple in Wakefield—Joseph Maleham and Frederica Lang. Enough glory for one day for one man! That last event may have quickened his own purposes, for the next year or so, it may be, I judge, he brought to his home at Simeon Dearborn's his young wife—her that was Mary Cutts of Portsmouth—and not long after moved a few steps to the new mansion which still stands on that site of remarkable beauty, which from that day to this has been the happy home of his descendants. Esquire Dearborn's house was near the road over Copp's hill. There was the "prophet's chamber" in the early day. And there they met and chose the first two deacons, Oct. 26, Simeon Dearborn, Esq., who had been deacon of the church in Greenland, and Avery Hall, formerly pastor at Rochester, from 1766 to 1775.

The church thus organized received additions from time to time, but the number was small, only two hundred for the century. The history of the church for the first quarter of a century is not very marked. No mighty revivals— convulsing society—when men quaked before the majesty and purity of God, but we may believe a steady stream of good influence was flowing on, blessing society. Later we find revivals, 1828, 1837, 1840, 1875, 1881. Then infant baptism was regarded important, and a few families consecrated their children, whose children's children are rejoicing in the God of their fathers. The first child baptized was William Maleham, whose parents, Joseph and Frederica, now took upon themselves vows to love the Lord, as they had vowed one year ago to love each other. Great grandchildren of Joseph Maleham are of this church, and in the

Sunday school the third and fourth generations, unto whom the Lord is showing mercy.

Richard Dow, one of the original members, became deacon, and in 1826 was, at his own request, relieved because of age and infirmity, and died in 1835, the same year as his pastor, full of years. His son, Asa, was one of the first to receive baptism. Several of his grand-children at this font were baptized, and to the memory of one of these, —who, sixty and four years ago, a babe in the arms of the aged minister, had placed upon her brow the sacred water— to her, as wife and mother, we owe the memorial of our Town Library and High School—Ellen Almira Dow, the mother of our honored friend—the daughter of Josiah, the grand-daughter of Richard Dow. Other descendants have been loyal to the church of God, with whom we share in regard for the Christians of that early day. Our communion set, also, is the gift of one who was here consecrated in infancy, and of her husband so recently called away. The grand-daughters of the first deacon are with us in a hale old age, still interested, as always, with other grand-children, in the service of the sanctuary. Descendants of the second deacon are not in town. But the early records show *him* holding the office of Town Clerk and first selectman for several years, and prominent in civil as in religious affairs— Avery Hall. He died in 1820, at the advanced age of eighty-two. The son of the first minister, Edward Cutts Piper, as deacon for nearly half a century, and the father as minister up to that time, cover nearly the whole hundred years of the church as office bearers. He quietly passed away in the month of February, 1881, just ninety years from that winter month when he was consecrated to God. Of him it is written: "He was the good old deacon, permitted for more than half a century to embellish in his ancestral home, a hard working farmer's life with the culture of a Christian gentleman. He had an apostolic beauty of character, and led a blameless life." Other deacons, Luther Dearborn, 1826; Asa Piper Wiggin,—and since 1879,

Satchel Weeks.

In several who became members of the little band, the promise was fulfilled, "With long life will I satisfy him." Thus, Dea. Dow covered fifty years of church life, as did the late Dea. Piper, who joined in 1831. At the same time joined Belinda Evans, now living in Ossipee as Mrs. Isaac Thurston, and Emily Peare, later, Rollins. The same year Mrs. Lucy Bradbury Chesley entered upon those 52 years of living in Wakefield as a member of this church, which ended only last year, when she sank to sleep on Easter day, at the age of ninety. Mrs. Rhoda Hobbs completes her half century in January. Yet, of the five original male members, two, and perhaps three, died within eighteen months after they joined the little band, Deacons Hall and Dow surviving Simeon Dearborn, Mayhew Clark and Samuel Haines.

Two of the members have become ministers,—John H. Mordough ('31) ord. Evang. '36, and serving the revived and reorganized church at Effingham for some three years prior to 1839. He died in 1869. Jonathan Byron Cook, son of Benjamin, as a lad of eleven, by the side of the village lawyer, joined the church in 1839, Sept. 8 ; settled as colleague pastor with Rev. Joshua Dodge, at Moultonboro', 1850-54 ; for several years, until very recently, at Hebron, N. H. Dr. Charles Coffin Barker, son of the revered minister, though never a member of this church, for some years has labored for his Master as a preacher of the Adventist faith.

Few have gone forth to win renown, whose names are on the church book. We cannot measure either the direct or indirect influence of the church upon this community in upbuilding morality and education, as well as spirituality. But the record is on high. The presence of the church, even with a small nominal membership, has acted as a restraining influence to keep back from impiety and wickedness. Like a tower of granite it has stood as a protest against sin ; and as a beacon tower to guide to a better and happier life.

It has not only introduced into the kingdom of heaven, but has introduced into or encouraged people to enter the kingdom of wisdom. Its early preachers were men of sound learning, educated in brain and heart, and, without doubt, roused by their scholarly productions in the pulpit, and out of it by their interest in education, an ambition among the lads of Wakefield, to secure that of more value than gold. The ministers supplemented the work of the near relatives, who were themselves college learned. With an illiterate minister, the boys, very likely, would have gone to school. But the early settlers in this vicinity did not want that kind. In some towns the parish minister was the only educated man. Not so in Wakefield. College graduates Wakefield had right along, even if the soil was rugged. From a list prepared, I find that some thirty have been at Exeter Academy, and most went to college, and I am sure that at Dartmouth, Harvard, Bowdoin and Yale not a few graduates hailed from Wakefield, not to speak of those other graduates, sons of other towns, who have entered the bowers of our Edens, and have carried off the fair daughters of Wakefield.

The physicians and lawyers of Wakefield have been educated men—those legal lights in the old days, Sawyer and Copp and Hobbs, and the son, not less talented, the later Sawyer, and Charles Chesley. The doctors,—Thomas Lindsey, who, before this century begun, wasn't always so successful with his minister's tax-list as in his practice, and his son, Thomas, Jr., Russell and Grant, Gilman and Swasey, McCrillis, Twitchell and Roberts; these men have been influential in the town and in the state. And they thought it no detriment to their minds to sit under the preaching of Parsons Piper and Barker, and receive instruction in divine things. The founders wanted a learned, orthodox ministry. Their descendants may have thought more of the "learned" than the "orthodox" part. But in getting the one they got the other. That by the by. Still we can claim as a church and congregation, some credit for the superior educational influences of this village in the past, through the pulpit and the pews. For years, in the vicinity of 1810. Parson Piper was President of the Trustees of Wolfeboro' Academy, and some of our boys wended their way thither, and some to Dow Academy about 1815. He was also of our Town committee, and may have fitted some for college. Parson Barker, in the first years of his Wakefield life, was principal of the Wakefield Academy in its palmiest days, with his gifted wife, once Katharine Knight, of Boscawen, as assistant, and for many years within your memory, supervisor of schools, giving each year reports prepared with great pains, serving his town even up to four score and three.

Wakefield Academy, since 1832, has had two or three lives, with temporary deaths intervening. Its room has been over the church room, to fulfil the conditions of a gift. But we would not put, in our lives, education in a room above religion. Either, alone, loses part of its power. Religion, all theory and no practice, or all emotion and no intelligence, is very hard and brittle, or very soft and transitory. If our church fathers erred, it was not in the latter. If they emphasized the intellect in the pulpit, it was because they feared a religion of pulp. If we are wiser than they, experience has been our schoolmaster. Perhaps if they had been milder, and put more of emotion into their scholarly sermons, and their views of life, they might have gained a larger number of additions, and reached more hearts. They were inflexible, that is, "set",—sometimes a virtue, sometimes a hindrance. This may account for small membership. Again, the church was virtually the state in a religious capacity, providing, as its duty, preaching at the central place, at the expense of the town, and each man on the grand list taxed. To this the majority assented. A few protested, but perhaps not more than would oppose other acts of the majority, such as a new road. Their protest was noticed. The sentiment grew quite strong against "taxation without representation", in this sense, that the preaching didn't express their views,—from some near the church as well as more remote. Some preferred preaching of a different sort, and some, then as now, probably preferred no preaching, and didn't wish to pay for the support of any highway they didn't travel on. There was also an idea that the minister should not be a "hireling." Still, if anything was to be given, let it be voluntary, not by taxing. As early as 1788, within three years from the settling of the first minister, several "who called themselves a Baptist Society" the town voted "to exempt from paying a tax to the town minister, and shall hold them excused so long as they support preaching among themselves according to their perswasion, or attend upon the ministry in their way; and at the same time, we wish their attendance with us, and leave it to their generosity to contribute what they please for the support of Mr. Piper." Their names will interest you: Samuel Allen, Samuel Allen, Jr., Ebenezer Cook, John Horn, the first town clerk, John Hill, Jacob Wiggin, Simeon Wiggin, Isaiah Wiggin, and Tobias Hanson. This was, I judge, the society later worshiping at the Spinney meeting house. In this neighborhood was the early home of that venerable minister, who, for full fifty years, has been almost our Town Minister, so wide has been his circuit and influence, and I regret to-day that he is not present, as I hoped he would be, to speak of olden days. I refer to Elder Joseph Spinney, of winning ways, and the appearance of a patriarch. Each year, nearly, some were excused. But the *town* only could excuse. It held that right, as well as to tax. It may not be proper for us, at this time, to criticise too sharply this right. We do not meet to-day to say that the First church should have remained the only one. But to rejoice that the good Lord permitted a FIRST church to exist in Wakefield. A variety in religious, as in political views, may be expected, even among a small population. Each view may be of hearts loyal to God or to the nation. And this variety is shown in the history of our town, as the number excused grew larger. In 1788, these ten I have mentioned; in 1794, fifteen; 1798, 37 out of 162 voters; 1804, 44; 1807, 98 out of 192, over one-half; 1810, the "contract" was "dissolved",—and, practically, from that time on, support was voluntary, Asa Piper not being the paid minister of the town, but pastor of the church for another quarter of a century, until, in 1819, Taxation for preaching was abolished by the "Act of Toleration". Dr. Lyman Beecher, one of the most eminent Orthodox divines then living, in his own state of Connecticut, earnestly and bitterly opposed that Act. He thought that the Restraint or Constraint of the Law taken away, the flood-gates would be opened, and a great tide of ungodliness sweep the villages. But the Lord lived. And Lyman Beecher lived to become an equally earnest advocate of Voluntary Support. Let us give our fathers credit for sincerity, whether they advocated the one or the other, and unite with such of them as believed that the Religious and Moral welfare of a Town is of the first importance. To them be honor given by us, their descendants,—to those "who came into the wilderness and left it a fruitful field"; who made homes for themselves and for us. The town improved in the quarter century when they had their First and only Town Minister. This is shown in the eloquent and pathetic document when Parson Piper on his part dissolved the contract, January 1st, 1810.

"The five and twentieth year is now in part elapsed since my induction into the important and sacred office of a religious Teacher in this place. At that time the people were few in number, and had but imperfectly subdued a wilderness, and prepared the soil to yield support to the inhabitants, who, being collected together from various places, were, many of them, far from abounding with the conveniences and delicacies of life. * * * * * * Fears were entertained by some at that time that the people would not be able to fulfil their engagements without bringing poverty and distress upon themselves. But a present view of the case will show how groundless were those fears. Instead of these temporary, humble cottages first erected, and which they would now think could scarce give shelter to their herds, we now behold comfortable and even elegant habitations. Thus hath a kind providence blessed us; and thus is there exhibited unto my eyes irresistible proof that what I have received from the town hath not impoverished them. In justice to myself, I must say, that I have ever cherished a lively sympathy with the people, and made it my constant endeavor to lighten the burdens, and not forget the poor. In all their afflictions I was afflicted; and an omnipresent Deity can witness my secret intercessions for unity, happiness and spiritual welfare of all. * * * * * * * Desirous as I am of meeting the wishes of the people, I have uniformly declared my readiness to absolve them from every obligation to contribute to my support, whenever they should express such a desire; and had such an event taken place several years ago rather than at this time, the probability is that it would have been more for my temporal happiness. Because, having expended a considerable sum in fencing and subduing my farm, and the like, I shall probably not find any one disposed to compensate me, should it become expedient to dispose of my property. Besides, the season of gray hairs admonishes me of approaching infirmities, and darkens the prospect before me. Nevertheless, I should prefer a "dinner of herbs where love is, unto a stalled ox and hatred therewith." It has lately been signified to me that a dissolution of the contract is wished for by some, and thought expedient by many. I do not feel disposed to throw obstacles in the way; and therefore declare my readiness to dissolve the civil contract. I would, therefore, say that I will agree unto its dissolution on the following conditions: 1st. That all sums now assessed by virtue of the contract be paid in conformity to its provisions. 2d. That I enjoy all immunities, as heretofore, while my relation to the church shall continue. 3d. That I receive, as an indemnification in part, for this concession, four hundred dollars.

To the inhabitants of the Town of Wakefield, this day in Town meeting assembled.

January 1st, 1810.                                    ASA PIPER.

At that town meeting, Maj. Joshua G. Hall moderator, it was voted to dissolve the contract according to Mr. Piper's proposals,—Joseph Wiggin, Town Clerk.

Thus. in 1810, the town ceased to support preaching, but the Town Minister continued as pastor for twenty-five years more, with a colleague from 1828 to 1833, until his death in 1835, much lamented. Old people now living, remember "the old priest", as he was called, and delight to tell of him, a man of massive frame, great dignity and upright character, who did much to up-build society in this town. To Parson Piper, the best citizen regarded not only the material, but the moral and spiritual interests of society. The best citizen wants the best roads and bridges, the best schools and churches. He himself was not purely a preacher on the Sabbath and secluded from society the rest of the week. He was a citizen, and one of the best. He was always at the polls, and his fellow citizens parted as he marched up through with stately step to deposit his ballot. He admired Washington. He was a leader in making improvements in husbandry. He beautified his own premises, lifting agriculture out of the rudimental condition, and sought to combine the beautiful with the useful. He believed in the elevating influence of nature, yet he wanted to transform the places "where every prospect pleases, and only man is vile". He cultivated the rugged soil, and aimed to please the eye as well as the appetite. We are not to get enjoyment by feeding upon fish and fowl alone, but feast the eye upon the rich foliage, and listen to the songs of the birds, and admire the heavens of beauty.

"Forever singing as they shine,
The hand that made us was divine."

Mr Piper made the address at the first agricultural Fair in this region, at Rochester, and the splendid shade trees planted by his hand, are a monument to his foresight, as they adorn the avenue in front of the ancestral grounds. He was a graduate of Harvard college, and his influence upon the town in those early days we may not fully know. The Circulating Library he was foremost in starting in 1797, which existed 60 years and then went out, only one shareholder now surviving in town—Hubartis Neal.

The record of our first minister, Asa Piper, the angels of Him who knows have kept. So our record is being written by unseen hands; and a hundred years from today, those now unborn may be recounting our deeds to our children's children. Let us keep the lights burning in the watch tower of Zion; and may the Sanctuary ever be the center of our life and prosperity in the home and in the town. To-day we are looking back over the generations of the past. It is valuable to do this; to keep in memory the deeds of those who toiled to subdue the forest, and cause the soil to bear fruit for man. The pioneers of our country did a great work, and deserve to be remembered, and remembered with gratitude. And they did that work because they had great souls, that were not daunted by any obstacles, who feared not the lions in the way, because they were stout hearted. And they left the impress upon their descendants. The nearer we get to them the more of this spirit do we have. Contact with rugged soil, and other things rugged, does not, of necessity, make the rugged, vigorous character. But the rugged character finds its congenial work in battling with the obstacles in nature and in man. Whoever can trace his ancestry back to one of those great-hearted families has an inheritance worth more than great riches. It might be well if circumstances now demanded that we should have to battle as did our fathers, and *use* our energies, not in developing shrewdness of character, but solidity.

So, to-day, let us seek, not merely for information about our fathers, but also inspiration from what they did, the the better ourselves to do the duty God lays upon us; so that we may leave—not footprints on the sands of time, which may be washed away,—but carve our names high up among the benefactors of humanity. The heroic spirit of our ancestors should be to each for an inspiration and a strength. But we cannot live simply on the heritage of the past. It is not good for a young man to live only on what his father leaves him. Each age toils and suffers for the next. The Pilgrim Fathers fled for "liberty" to a new land, and suffered. Then the Revolutionary Fathers *fought* and bled for "liberty". Our Farmer Fathers toiled to preserve that "liberty".—And what shall we do? We must toil for the next century, and so each one shall have a heritage to which he can add by his toil. We have a free country, a Christian land. The Bible is not sealed. The school houses are not burned down. Our houses of worship are abundant, and the gospel is helping us on to a better and happier life. The Lord be thanked that that seed was planted in 1785. We have a right to sing the song of the tiny acorn, and then go forth to help to make the new century, more than any other since the world began, God's century, and years of the right hand of the Most High.

Hon. Seth Low was next introduced by the President, and spoke as follows:

Mr. Chairman and Citizens of Wakefield:

"As shadows chased by cloud and sun
  Fly fitful o'er the grass,
So in thy sight, Almighty One,
  The generations pass.

Standing here to-day as the son of Ellen Almira Dow, whose father was Josiah Dow, and whose grandfather was Richard Dow, all of whom were identified with this place, and all of whom long since have been gathered to their fathers, I am reminded with peculiar solemnity of these lines of the New England poet. This Richard Dow was one of the original members of the first church of Wakefield, whose Centennial we celebrate to-day; therefore I have a right to be with you at this time, a right which also I value as a privilege. Whether it is due or not to the stream of New Hampshire blood that runs in my veins I cannot tell, but certain it is that though a dweller in the city, I never read without a responsive tingle which I can feel, that old psalm of Israel's poet King, "I will lift up mine eyes unto the hills from whence cometh my help." The up-lift of the mountains upon the soul of man, as they point him sky-ward, seems to me a very real thing. I often wonder whether you who dwell beneath the calm, far gaze of the mountains themselves, feel this as the children of New Hampshire feel it when they see the mountains only now and then. In any case, I am glad to be with you to-day, to join you in blessing God that He put it into the hearts of your fathers and mine one hundred years ago, to found this first church of

Wakefield. Those of us who live in cities learn that all men do not see things in the same way. Neighbors differ on every question that comes up. They differ in taste and in general make-up, no less than in ideas. We see about us there, men of other birth trained under different customs; and we learn, or ought to learn, that no one man and no one nation posesses all that is good, or all that is true. So in our churches, we ought to learn, I conceive, that no one church and no one kind of a church contains the whole truth and the power to commend it to all men. I am not indifferent to the evils that come from the divisions among Christians, but I plead for recognition of the unity that lies back of the divisions. Men tell us, you know, that all the colors of the rainbow are contained within a ray of white light, but the world is lit, not by the rays divided into colors, nor yet by light devoid of separate colors; but the "light which lighteth every man which cometh into the world," is a light in which all partial lights are so blended as to make the perfect ray of universal brightness. So it is that some of us, born of this old New Hampshire strain, worship the God of our fathers in a fashion different from that which was dear to them. But we, no less than you, worship the same God, and we try, as you do, to worship him in spirit and in truth. So I ask you to believe of the little church at the Junction, which is very dear to me and to others who hold precious the names of many who have worshiped in your midst in this old Corner Church, I ask you to believe of that little church at the Junction that we worship there the same God as our fathers did, and that we desire to do it in the fullest fellowship with you of devotion to a common Lord. I am glad with all my heart to see present to-day, and taking part in these services, the Rector of that church, for well I know that if God had not given to Richard Dow one hundred years ago a heart which led him to join in the establishment of this First church of Wakefield, there is little chance that his descendants would have cared to help to establish any church in this or in any place. I hail you, therefore, gladly, as is your due, as the Mother Church of Wakefield ; and as one of those who feel this obligation to you for your past, I bid you God-speed for a fortunate and useful future, and I bespeak, as between you and your daughter church at the Junction, that unity and fellowship of feeling which is born of consecration to the service of one God and one Lord.

The President next introduced Miss Harriet N. Hobbs who read the following poem written by her for the occasion :

## HIS MESSAGE.

As in the silence of an unused room
   We idly stay our weary feet,
Watching where in the stillness and the gloom
   The shadows and the sunshine meet,

Through ways of mystery we come to know
   Our dead are waiting with us there,
Moving with noiseless footsteps to and fro
   An unseen presence in the air.

"We hold the secret of eternal years"
   They softly whisper and pass by,
"Lo to the happy dead can come no tears,
   The best of life is, we may die."

Oh church of God with century blossom crowned
   To day doth lead us into space
By grim shadows peopled, who by no sound
   Do break the silence of their place.

Through the vibrant air the soul hears the call
   In Eden, and the answered shame
Burdened with weight of life and death to all,
   As there the shadowed promise came.

Under the noontide heat on Mamre's plain
   In his tent door watching his flocks,
Mourning the years he has waited in vain
   For Shiloh, while doubting Sarah mocks,

As through the mists of early morning light
  We see climbing with faith sublime
Up the rough steeps of Moriah's height
  The patriarch of olden time.

From far off Nebo gazing down, his face
  Radiant with the dawning light
Of heaven, Moses sees God's chosen race
  Waiting to take their promised right.

For them grapes of Eschol who know no taste
  Of earthly food.  For them a land,
Erewhile they wandered over desert waste,
  A murmuring rebellious band.

Wearing her heaped mantle with stately pride
  Softly the heathen gleaner sings
Through the Judean fields at eventide
  The mother of Israel's kings.

As the swift after ages move along
  With full cycles, in sure accord        .
Out of the hill country comes Mary's song
  "My soul doth magnify the Lord".

But as a wayward child afar off flings
  As he stands with averted face
The better gift a loving father brings
  To take some childish vision's place.

Amid the nations doth Israel stand
  As one seeing, yet will not see
The daystar bringing to a waiting land
  The coming day of prophecy.

Their ears are heavy when the bitter cry
  From Him grief stricken and thorn crowned
Sweeps through the world, "It is finished, I die
  Smitten and pierced by many a wound.

Behold me I came to my own in vain.
  For all the love I gave to them,
They gave me scorn and stripes and bitter pain.
  And yet of old in Bethlehem

Prophets found for me a habitation,
   And there arose that wondrous star
The hope of ancient Israel's nation
   Which wise men worshipped from afar.

I had reigned for aye when the world was young
   A king upon my Father's throne,
Or ere the morning stars together sung
   I claimed this people for my own.

Oppressed I stood before my slayers dumb.
   To you of Gentile race my word
I give, to speak through ages yet to come
   The message of thy risen Lord.

Fear not the task, I am with you alway.
   As of old I am shield and light.
A brooding and shadowy cloud by day,
   A bright and guiding flame by night.

I will lead thee in paths thou hast not known,
   Oh my beloved follow me.
I know thee and I shall not lose my own,
   However rough the way may be.

Thou must struggle to many a Calvary
   Bearing the cross over the way,
But remember that I went before thee
   In anguish, on that awful day.

When even my Father had hid His face
   From me, and through the darkened land
All the righteous dead from their resting place
   Arose, and walked, a ghastly band.

Go forth and work until that day of rest
   When an exultant throng shall sing
"Their works do follow them, and they are blest.
   Lo the Lamb who was slain is King."

To the harvest for the eternal years
   Some that day will bear ripened sheaves,
And others trembling and with bitter tears
   Can bring me only withered leaves.

Throughout the livelong  day all bravely toil.
  But when at last the night is come,
Some joyful bring the victor's spoil
  And some with folded hands are dumb.
But she who touched my garment's hem
  Was healed.  So mourning hearts, be still
For God His grace divine will give to them
  Simply content to do His will.
And in His city that glorious day
  Lo all my ransomed church shall meet
Before my Father's throne to dwell alway
  And there to worship at His feet.

At the after dinner informal service at the  meeting house
Hon. J. G. Hall was called upon to  give, in  regard to the
early settlers, some

## "REMINISCENCES."

My Friends, this Centennial observance of the embodi-
ment of the Congregational Church in Wakefield and the
ordination of its first Pastor is to us all a day of stirring
memories.  In years to come we shall ever recur to it as a
memorable day and its recollections will be a delight to us
to the close of life.  In my own case the occasion reminds
me that my ancestors, both paternal and maternal, have,
from the earliest settlements at Dover and Newbury without exception or break in the descending lines to this day
adhered to the old Congregational views, and I take satisfaction in being a member of the old Parish where the first
ancestor this side the sea of my Friend the President of the

day and myself, officiated as the first deacon of the church and where in the words of the old Dover records of the year 1671 he "agried with the Selectmen to sweep the Meetinghouse and ring the bell for one holl yeir & to have for that sarves the some of three pounds."

But this ancient church true to the tolerant spirit that its first Pastor and his flock manifested for those whose religious opinions differed from theirs, walking in the ways of Christian fellowship with those of other faiths, enlarge their borders to-day and ask all the Town to come in and with them once again as of old for one day at least be one fold ; so that this is the Centennial of the Town as well as of the Church and this is as it should be, for though one hundred years ago this Town and this Church were by no means co-incident as they were at an earlier period in Massachusetts still the church here bore to the Town very much the relation that the soul does to the body. It was indeed the light set on the hill. Had the early settlers been told that they must maintain the Town without the church they would have abandoned their homes here and gone elsewhere where they could have had the gospel preached. In brief, the church our Fathers planted here and those that have grown up in its shadow have made the Town and it is fitting that we should all come in and celebrate with this Mother church her centennial day. The occasion is fruitful in suggestion to us all and it specially reminds *me* that we have been remiss in our duty to our ancestors, to ourselves and to posterity alike in not causing a history of the town to be written and published. The history of Wakefield ought to have been written years ago. Had some one of our citizens of fifty or even forty years ago undertaken the work we might to-day possess a volume at once instructive and grateful to the mind of this generation and of those who may succeed us. Among the first settlers and the generations following there was an exceptionally large proportion of strong minded and intelligent men and women. Superior as they were in mental grip and acquired knowledge they exercised a controlling force and impressed themselves on the people of the surrounding country. Their lives were abundant in stirring incidents that would have greatly enriched the pages of a Town history. But busy as the men of three score years ago were in the struggle for bread and a little learning for their children no time was found nor thought given to garnering the deeds of our early days for the delight and profit of their descendants, and so I fear much of the most valuable material for a history of the Town is lost irrevocably. Still, that time and labor will give us a history of great interest and value even at this late day, the able and discriminating historical discourse of your Pastor this morning is gratifying evidence. If this occasion is of no other service than to excite such an interest in our ancestors as will lead speedily to the writing of the story of their lives posterity I am sure will refer to it as a red letter day in the Town's life. The limits of Wakefield remain the same as when the town was incorporated excepting that the small portion above Province Pond was in 1820 annexed to Effingham, but I find that in 1820 an effort was made by the people living in this town below Lovell's pond with others living in the Northerly part of Milton, to have that part of Wakefield south of Lovell's pond and the northerly portion of Milton incorporated into a new town. Luther Dearborn of this town and John Remick Jr. of Milton headed petitions to the legislature for the new town which was to be called Lisbon. The Rev. Mr. Piper favored the project and suggested the name Milfield for the new town. This town fell within the limits of the Masonian patent and as appears by the records of the Masonian Proprietors, a company of wealthy Portsmouth gentlemen who had some time before bought of Mason's heirs their interest in the land covered by the Masonian patent, at a meeting holden in Portsmouth April 27th 1749 the Township now called Wakefield, but then known as East Town was granted by vote to John Ham, Gershom Downs, John Horn and seventy-six others all described as being residents of Dover and Somersworth with the one ex-

ception of Noah Emery of Kittery Maine. By the terms
of this grant the land was divided into one hundred shares
and each lot of land was to contain when surveyed one
hundred acres. Further provisions and conditions on which
the grant was made were that one of the shares should be
for the first minister of the Gospel who might be settled in
in the town and continue here during his life or until regular-
ly dismissed. That another of said shares should be for the
support of the Gospel Ministry, that the one hundred acre
lots belonging to these shares should be laid out as near the
place where the meeting-house might be built as may be
conveniently done. That there be six acres of land left in
some convenient place for building a meeting-house and
school-house upon, and to be used as a training field, a
burying place or other public uses as the inhabitants may
have occasion to improve it for. That one other of said
shares shall be for the use and maintainance of a school forever. It was farther provided that the grantees should settle thirty families in town within four years after the close
of the war then raging between the English, and the French
and Indians, each family to have a house at least sixteen
feet square and three acres of land cleared and fitted for
mowing and tillage, and that ten more families should be
settled by the end of five years from the close of the war
and that within six years from the declaration of Peace a
meeting-house should be built and that the preaching of the
Gospel should be maintained from the end of seven years.
It appears further from the Masonian records which are in
the custody of the descendants of the last proprietor's Clerk
at Portsmouth, that the lots were drawn in Portsmouth at
Ann Slayton's Inn, April 11, 1750. Out of the seventy-
nine who received the grant of the town I find less than a
dozen whose family name is the same with that of any of
the old settlers here. I doubt if half a dozen ever settled
here. I recognize in the list many who were a hundred
and fifty years ago prominent in Dover and Somersworth.
Among them was Col. Paul Gerrish who was in his time

a foremost man in Dover, one so much revered and honored
that when he died, his Pastor the Rev. Jonathan Cushing
says that near one thousand persons attended his funeral.
These men purchased the town not for settlement themselves but for speculation, and this leads me to say that the
makeup of this town was essentially different from that of
the Massachusetts towns and even the older towns of southern New Hampshire. This difference was partly the result
of the more recent time when the first settlement was made
here and partly of the different causes which brought our
Fathers here. In Massachusetts, in Hampton, Dover, Exeter and Derry the town and church were coincident. Portsmouth was an exception because the headquarters of the
Provincial government was there and of course the English
Church thus early had a foothold and somewhat disputed
the ground with the Puritans. Neither in this nor any other town in New Hampshire settled in the last half of the last
century were church and town coincident, and church membership was never here made a prerequisite for holding civil office as was the case at one time in Massachusetts. The
first settlers did not come here for greater freedom of worship. They were not English emigrants fleeing from the
persecution of a State church, but they were the hardy, ad-
venturous young and middle aged men from the older towns
of the Province where they and their Fathers for more than
a hundred years had enjoyed all the religious freedom that
Brewster and the Plymouth colony or Winthrop and his
followers hoped for or desired when they first set foot on
New England soil; and while the acts of the first settlers
here in setting up public worship and maintaining the ordinances of the church attest their loyalty to the Christian
faith as held by the early settlers of New England, their
primary object in coming here I imagine, was to better
their worldly condition. Dover, Exeter, Hampton, Portsmouth, and Newbury after they had been settled one hundred years seemed to the active young men of 1760 to be
getting thickly peopled. The best of the pine and the oak

had been cut down. With succeeding generations and increasing numbers the farms had been divided and subdivided until the young and enterprising turned their thoughts to newer lands and to what seemed broader and easier avenues to wealth. The Masonian proprietors were surveying their lands in this region and offering them for sale. Visions of wealth loomed up to some from the pine forests of the Salmon Falls and Saco valleys, to others the thought of possessing broad acres and founding a new estate was a fascination, and so the young and stalwart from the older settlements below us came and settled this town and founded this church. Now while all the early settlers here were not sample Pilgrims like Brewster and Bradford at Plymouth nor Puritans like Winthrop and Endicott of Massachusetts Bay they had all been trained more or less in Puritan ways and were so far as we can tell by the church records in the towns whence they came hither the baptized children of the church. Not a man of them but reverenced the ways of religion as it had been taught to them. They reverenced the Sanctuary and were in their place there on the Sabbath. They were generally deeply religious men and women, and so at an early day, as soon as they were strong enough in numbers, a minister was settled and a church formed. Our Fathers were fortunate in the selection of their first religious teacher. At the time of Mr. Piper's settlement here you are aware that the minister was the most important person in the town. No one else approached him in dignity or influence. He always had the opportunity, if he possessed the requisite character and force of intellect, to mould the sentiment of his parish greatly to his liking. I think from all I can learn from those now living who remember him well that Mr. Piper was never an aggressive man and he was the farthest remove from a domineering parson, but he came here well fitted by nature and education to exercise a lasting and most happy influence upon the town and he did it in a gentle and effective way. He was large of stature, of a good presence, dignified in his bearing always, a model of propriety on all occasions. So far as I can learn, no one ever charged him with indiscretion of word or mien. He was fortunate in his lineage, for, as you have been told to-day, he came of sound English stock. He was equally fortunate in the place of his birth and in the time and events amid which his childhood was passed. It is good fortune to any one to have been born in old Middlesex, in the shadow of Bunker Hill in sight of the fields of Concord or the Lexington meadows; anywhere in the fields and mansions of old Middlesex. Nowhere in the old thirteen colonies was there more intelligent love and daring for independence than in Middlesex county and nowhere was the patriotic feeling more intense than in the quiet town of Acton where Mr. Piper was born and reared. It was the Acton minute men who at daybreak on the 19th day of April 1775 "crowded at the drum beat to the house of Isaac Davis their captain who made haste to be ready." Later in the day this Acton company formed on the right of the line at the old north bridge at Concord and it was this company that received the first volley from the British regulars in the battle of that day by which their captain and Abner Hosmer a son of one of the deacons in the church in Acton fell dead, and before night the son of another deacon, James Hayward, had fallen while pursuing the British army in their retreat to Boston. Mr. Piper was not in this service and he may have been at the University at Cambridge where he was then a student. But doubtless he directly after passed up the high road to Concord, the route taken by the British army on the 19th of April, on the way to the funeral of his father's neighbors who had fallen at Concord. On the road he might have seen the spot where Haynes, a deacon of the church in Sudbury, fell at the age of eighty years while fighting the British in their retreat through Lexington, and the thickets and stone walls at the high land in Lincoln where the Americans made such havoc in the ranks of the retreating English, and captured their leader, Major Pitcairn, he must have observed, and doubtless he was one of that concourse of neighbors from miles around who followed to the village graveyard in Acton the remains of Davis and Hosmer and others of his father's neighbors and some of them perhaps his kinsmen who had fallen in that first day's fight for civil liberty to the colonies. While a student at Cambridge he must have heard the impassioned appeals of Samuel Adams and Warren in the old South Meeting House in Boston. Hancock must have been a familiar figure to him for he was much in Cambridge in those days and perhaps he saw Washington draw his sword under the ancient elm in Cambridge and very likely he heard Jeremy Belknap, then the minister at Dover, as he preached to the army in the streets of Cambridge. These scenes and the high companionship of patriots and martyrs for the cause of civil liberty moulded our first pastor greatly for his whole future life; and you do not wonder when I tell you that those who knew him best here recall that he always took a lively interest in public affairs, that he always had strong political feeling, that he loved the discussion of public measures before the country for the time being. He was never a politician. His clerical office and his elevated views saved him from that fate. Like most of the Congregational clergy of his time he was a Federalist holding Washington in the highest veneration, a firm believer in the policy of Hamilton and Adams, and dsiliking the notion of Jefferson and dreading the influence of his views on questions of public policy because in connection with his associates in the ministry he thought him a deist and perhaps an atheist and that the success of his party foreboded a repetition to some extent at least of the scenes of the then recent French revolution. Through all his active life I judge Mr. Piper was not averse, to say the least, to political discussion in a quiet way when a proper occasion offered itself. Sometime while the late Hon. Nathaniel Upham of Rochester, himself the son of the minister of Deerfield, was a member of Congress and perhaps about 1820, Mr. Upham called early in the day at the store then standing opposite the "Old Maid's Tavern" where he found his friend parson Piper. Mr. Upham was fresh from a session of Congress and very soon he and the minister were in earnest political discussion which was kept up till near night when Mr. Upham remarked that he must be on his way to a store he then owned, either on Copp's hill or at Wakefield corner I am not sure which, but that if Mr. Piper desired he would renew the discussion the next day at his store. The suggestion was promptly accepted and the discussion went on at Mr. Upham's store for two days more in the presence of several of Mr. Piper's neighbors. Perhaps no one is now living who listened to this three days of political talk, but I years ago had a full account of it from one who listened from beginning to end of it, and more recently upon enquiry of my lamented and venerable friend Luther Dearborn Sawyer who died last year at the age of eighty, he told me that he remembered perfectly well listening the last two days of the discussion.

Of the committee of seven who signed the call to Mr. Piper to settle in the ministry, one was Capt. Jeremiah Gilman who came with his family to Wakefield perhaps as early as 1767 and built his house just opposite the "Old Maid's Tavern" where he lived up to the time of his death in 1791, his farm extending from the highway westerly to the river. This man was born at Exeter June 3rd 1719 whence he removed to this town. His father Andrew Gilman and an uncle Jeremy Gilman were taken prisoners by the Indians while at work in a saw-mill at "Pickpocket" in Exeter in the spring of 1709. Andrew eventually escaped from his captors and returned home. Naturally the son imbibed some dislike to the Indians and doubtless the only good Indian to him was a dead Indian. At any rate he was an Indian fighter and a captain in the old French and Indian war. He marched armed with gun and sword, adopting largely the Indian methods of fighting. Among the incidents of his soldier life he used to relate that at one time, exhausted by the heat, and protracted fighting he quenched his thirst by drinking from a pool ot water reddened by the blood of the combatants. In 1777, when the descent of Burgoyne's army upon New York was imminent, he raised a company here, joined Stark's forces and took part in the battle of Bennington. At this time he was fifty-eight years of age, and his wife claiming that he had done his part as a soldier endeavored to persuade him not to again enter the service, but on a July afternoon the little company was formed in front of the captain's house, the captain stepping in front said "Come on boys" and all hands started down the road on the double quick, bivouacked that night in a barn in Rochester and marched thence to Exeter where they joined Gen. Stark's forces. After a desperate fight of two hours at Bennington the British intrenchments were carried, Gilman being as his soldiers said the second man to follow Stark over the breastworks of the enemy where a hand to hand conflict was terminated by the utter rout of the enemy. This Capt. Gilman with his cousin Lieut. Jonathan Gilman are I suppose the two Gilmans who are mentioned in a memorandum found among Mr. Piper's papers as the first families that wintered in town. Jonathan settled on the old main road from Wakefield to Milton nearly opposite the house of the late John Kimball. His descendants for three generations have owned and occupied the farm where his great-grandson Jonathan R. Gilman now resides on the road from Union Village to Brookfield. These men reckoned their descent from three of our Colonial governors—Gov. Andrew Wiggin, Gov. Simon Bradstreet, and Gov. Thomas Dudley. The man of the most prominence in civil affairs in the early days of the town was Capt. David Copp who lived where Hon. John W. Sanborn now resides. Coming here early from Rochester he seems for many years to have been the central figure in the management of public affairs. In wealth, social standing, and in influence he was the first man in the town. There was no office in the gift of the people he did not enjoy, and there was no call of his country that he was not among the foremost to obey. He was in command of a company at the Battle of Bunker Hill. Andrew Gilman was his first lieutenant. He was perhaps continuously in service to the close of the Revolution. Avery Hall one of the first deacons of this church was a native of Wallingford, Connecticut, a graduate of Yale college in 1759 and pastor of the church in Rochester from 1766 to 1775. Shortly after his dismission from the Rochester church he removed to this town and lived on the farm now owned by John Kimball where he died at the age of 82 in 1820. At Rochester, as the church records show, there was anything but harmony between him and some of his church. For years the records allude to the pending strife and at last a large council of the neighboring churches very reluctantly, apparently, recommended a dissolution of the pastoral relation in a very lengthy and elaborate report, but so adroitly drawn as most effectually to conceal the reasons of the council, if they had any, for the conclusion reached. The *truth* was as I know from a most trustworthy source that Mr. Hall was in no fault at all, but a female member of his church who was a Scotch Presbyterian had conceived the notion that Mr. Hall was not as thoroughly Calvinistic as he ought to be, and being joined by a few others persisted in her opposition to him until the neighboring churches were induced for the sake of peace to recommend his dismission. After coming to this town Mr. Hall was much employed as a magistrate and was in his latter years known as Esquire Hall. He saw much trouble here, his faithful daughter Sally, always the light of the home and the aged father's main dependence after the mother's death, sickened and died, his house was burned, and in his last years his means were quite limited, but he died as he had lived a good man held in high esteem by all who knew him.

Perhaps no family is oftener spoken of or held in higher esteem by us than the Dow family, and I am quite sure none have done more for the religious and educational welfare of the town than Deacon Richard Dow one of the original members of this church, to whom fitting reference has been made to-day, and his descendants. Of the recent benefactions made here by his grand-children I may not speak in this presence, but I may properly remind you that his son Josiah Dow then a leading merchant of Boston in 1815 at his own expense built upon his father's farm a building, and established the Dow Academy which continued in operation till about 1820. Josiah Dow was a man in high business and social position. He took an active interest in the success of the school, and youth of both sexes from the surrounding country as well as from Boston, Salem, and the large towns of southern New Hampshire filled the schoolrooms. An ample teaching force of the best grade was provided by Mr. Dow and the Academy while it continued enjoyed a reputation hardly second to any in the state. It has been my good fortune to know several venerable men now dead, who were once students at Dow Academy. They were already advanced in years when I first talked with them, men learned in their professions, examples of good breeding and of high character. These men never tired of talking of their days spent at Dow Academy and there was no praise too high for them to bestow on its teachers and founder. They not only remembered the excellence of the work done daily in the large class-room but they delighted to dwell on the pomp and circumstance of exhibition days, which the Founder always attended and when they had martial music and a procession. The Academy was dedicated Nov. 6, 1815 when Mr. Dow delivered the address. Rev. Andrew Thayer was the first preceptor. In 1819 Mr. Adam Gordon, Miss Rebecca Phippen and Miss Eliza Bailey were the teachers, and at one time the late Hon. John Aiken of Andover, Mass., was a preceptor.

And so we recount the work of a few of that company who a hundred years ago to-day witnessed the settlement of the town's first religious teacher near the spot where many of them with that pastor lie buried. They meant to build well their little commonwealth. It was the town they founded just a little more than a century ago but it was not complete nor did it in any way satisfy them till just a hundred years ago this beautiful day they had founded a church and settled a minister of the Gospel. I trust that ere long the story of their lives may take shape in a town history, and that proper memorial stones may mark the place of the old meeting-house and the grave of their pastor.

The following Notes will guide some in our picturing of the early settlers already mentioned.—A. H. T.

1. Lt. Jona. Gilman of Exeter—the first settler in 1767 at the age of 47; in 1774, 53; in 1785, 66—served as Moderator and second Selectman in 1777.

2. Capt. Jere. Gilman, his cousin, at about the same date and age, was a warrior. Andrew, Capt. Copp's Lt., was his son.

3. John Horn, third settler, perhaps in 1768, in age not far from 30, one of the few original proprietors who settled in the township. Born in Dover and died in 1830 at 91, the oldest person in town. He lived on Witch-trot road in "Goudy field."

4. Benj. Perkins, from Dover Point, settled early on what is now the home place of Noah Kimball Nutter. Much interested in the improving of the burying-ground.

5 John Kimball, of Exeter, younger brother of Jona. Gilman's wife, when 27 bought in 1768 Lot 40, since owned by a son, Ward W. Third Selectman in 1776. He died about 1806. His brother (younger)

6. Noah Kimball, son-in-law of Jere. Gilman, living in East Town, bought the next lot 38 in 1770 when 26; first of 2d Selectmen, 1774; father of "Master John". Died in 1810 at 66.

7. Capt. David Copp (1738—1817) came from Rochester before 1770 when perhaps 30 years old; 46 when Mr. Piper came; first Moderator at 35, and for most of the next 15 years divided that honor with

8. Simeon Dearborn (1727—1787) who came from Greenland before 1770. He was also Justice of the Peace. His wife's brother, John Haven, came later and was an extensive land owner. Josiah Page bought of Simeon Dearborn in Sept. 1773, and lived near him. David Copp, William Moore, first constable, Daniel Hall and John Kimball, first school committee. '79 Jos. Leavitt bought Haven's house (opposite Dearborn's) for a tavern.

9. Joseph Maleham (1743—1816) first 3d Selectman at 31 in 1774.

10. John Wingate 3d and 2d Selectman six or seven years after 1780.

11. Lt. after Col. Jona. Palmer was younger than these but became later quite a prominent Federalist in the town and state. (1751—1843)

12. Nath'l Balch, first Deputy in Prov. Cong. at Exeter from Wakefield in 1775. He seems to have lived between John Horn on the west and on the east on Witch-trot road Eliphalet Quimby, the father of [13.] Dorothy—first child. From Exeter 1767.

14. Jacob Wiggin and [15.] Nathan Mordough, from Greenland, served on the board of Selectmen in early years. Also

16. Sam'l Hall who with his brother Dan'l Hall came early and was a land owner living near now A. S. Weeks'. Dan'l lived about opposite N Balch's

17. Avery Hall (1737—1820) came near 1776. Town clerk for ten years after John Horn. Also first Selectman '79 to '87, and a leader in the organizing of the church. Lived on site of Kimball Hotel.

18. Mayhew Clark of North Hampton bought of Capt. Copp in Lot 15 (on Tuttle's Hill) in May 1772. 3d Selectman 1781 to '84; 2d in 1780 and '85, and probably died in office, February 1786.

The male church members in order of age were

19. Samuel Haines, 69, the oldest, (1716) fourth by descent from Dea. Samuel Haines (England 1611) of the First Church in Portsmouth and one of its nine origi-

inal members, like his great grandson here in 1785. Not his but his son's wife joined the next year.

Simeon Dearborn, 57; Avery Hall, 47; Mayhew Clark, perhaps 38.

20. Richard Dow (1753—1835) 32, the youngest, came about 1780 from Kensington; later Deacon and the last survivor of the little band of 1785 fifty years after, when he died some three months before the minister

21. Rev. ASA PIPER, only 27,

born in Acton, Mass., Mar. 7, 1757, and died at Wakefield, May 19, 1835, at 78.

Mr. George S. Dorr, editor of the *Carroll County Pioneer*, at Wolfeboro' Junction, the latest addition to the villages of Wakefield, was asked to furnish a poem for the occasion, but owing to press of other business at the time, was unable to do so. The following lines, however, which appeared in the *Pioneer* as a part of Mr. Dorr's report of the proceedings of the day, the compiler deems fitting and proper to give a place in this work, and therefore, with permission, here inserts them :

Behind the dusty bars of time
Is rung to-day a century's chime;
A century dim, with all it holds,
To-day the grasping past enfolds.

We bid you all remember well
The struggles none may fully tell,
Of Parson Piper and the few,
Who "builded better than they knew".

O'er these hills their feet have trod,
Their ancient plows upturned this sod;
They builded homes, they churches raised,
Within whose walls their God they praised.

A century old—this church and town
Outlasts many a gilded crown;
To-day we place a golden star
Within Time's swift revolving car.

A golden clasp—this bright To-day—
Binds two centuries on our way;
Behind we hear a last faint chime
Mingle with that of coming time.

And may we, who stand to-day,
Where stood those long passed away,
Leave a record bright and pure,
Which, like theirs, shall long endure.

The compiler regrets his inability to present the pleasing address of fellowship of the next speaker, Rev. Wm. Lloyd Himes, of the Episcopal Church at Wolfeboro' Junction, but as he has received none of it for publication, the omission is unavoidable, and he passes on to the address of Rev. Gardner S. Butler of Union Village. Mr. Butler said:

I have reason to hold this church in grateful esteem since it is my privilege to care for her youngest daughter. Though small, she is a precious child, destined, I trust, to prove a blessing to the world, and an honor to her from whom she sprang. I also count it a favor to be here that I may receive an inspiration from the past. As we have heard recounted the noble work, wrought under difficulties by those who have preceded us, who has not received a fresh impulse to high endeavor? It was not in other lands, but here; not amid extraordinary scenes, but in the common walks of life, that our fathers lived and labored. Therefore, the history of their lives is more useful to us. The inspiring power of this day upon us is a reminder that we, too, may yet be an inspiration to those who shall take the places we now fill. A review of the past ought to arouse within us the spirit of gratitude. By hard labor did our fathers fell the forest and plant in its place the trees whose fruit we now enjoy. Our most essential blessings were left us by those who have gone before. We may select from what has been given us, and improve what we select; but we do not originate that which is most useful to us. It will take another generation to make useful what we create. The food we gather, unaided by those who precede us, is but manna. It is only when death has driven out the inhabitants whose place we take, that we eat the "Old corn of the land." If disposed to boast of the high position we now occupy, a glance downward over the past will reveal the fact that our ascent has been reached by steps our fathers laid. As well might the top stone of a pyramid boast over the stones that support it. They build unwisely who cast aside certain great foundation stones which have proved so secure in the past, or who undertake to trim the corners of those stones and thus make them insecure to build upon. There is apparent in the attitude of some among us a purpose to cast away, or so change as to render useless, some of the essential principles which our fathers taught. If unchecked, the sad results of such teaching must in time appear. The rough stones of Orthodoxy used by our fathers may need to be smoothed; but to round and polish them until they bear the name "Progressive Orthodoxy" will only serve to make them unfit for use. It is only a question of time when it shall be said of a church built on such a foundation, "Great was the fall of it." Hard as it might be for some of us to accept every doctrinal statement of the "Westminster Catechism", it is far better than a creed tinctured with the teaching of the "New Departure." The character formed by the teaching of this and other old New England churches must secure the respect of all who love right principles. Fill the leading pulpits and chief political positions of our country with men of the Puritanic stamp of character and our nation would have a great moral and general uplift.

Then was sung the anthem "Jerusalem my happy home", after which Rev. Sumner Clark was called upon. His address was mainly in the line of reminiscences. He alluded to the fact that his first visit to Wakefield was during the pastorate of Mr. Leffingwell. At that time he attended the meeting of the old Harmony Association, and preached in this house in the evening. His connection with former ministers had been somewhat peculiar. To borrow the language of Mr. Tappan, sustaining to him, at Marshfield and Wakefield, the relation of "successor, predecessor and successor." Rev. Mr. Barker was referred to as affording valuable aid in social services, particularly the Missionary Concert. At the close of his remarks Mr. Clark read the following, suggesting that "perhaps it might turn out a song, perhaps turn out a sermon".

Ecc. 7·10—Say not thou, what is the cause that the former days were better than these? for thou dost not inquire wisely concerning this.

" 'Tis distance lends enchantment to the view."
Thus wrote the Poet, and how clearly true.
The far remote in space is deemed most fair,
The far remote in time exceeding rare.
One only Paradise on earth we trace
At the commencement of the human race.
So in the pristine eras there were found
Both giant men, and mammoth beast, renowned.
Then, too, by ancient records it appears,
Some stretched their lives almost a thousand years.
Still, when we further read of murd'rous Cain,
And ruin dire on cities of the plain,
Of plagues inflicted by a righteous God,
Of tongues confounded, and o'erwhelming flood,
Of wars and exiles, and the many ills
With which all history its dark pages fills,
Strange would it be if any should deplore
They did not live in those same days of yore.
But coming nearer to the present time,
And leaving distant lands for our own clime,
'Tis no hard task to show that by-gone days
Were not entitled to superior praise.

Among the forests dense, all rough and wild,
Here careless lived free Nature's rougher child;
Of savage habits, and of hideous mien,
And mind more dark, the Indian might be seen.
True worship they had none, but, as they saw
In elements around some "higher law",
Ascribed the rule of all beneath the skies,
To a celestial Spirit great and wise,
Whose angry frown in storms and winds appear,
His smiling face in waters bright and clear.
At length by force of jealousy and war,
The different tribes were scattered wide and far.
Yet not henceforth to desolation drear
Was left this spot so fraught with beauty's cheer.
Another race, with resolution strong
To guard the right, and overthrow the wrong,
Here built their dwellings, and with patient toil,
The forests cleared, and subdued the soil.
Foundations laid with energy and zeal,
Both for their civil and religious weal.
But, turning now to this our goodly town,
And noting well the objects of renown,
But few of all the varied things now seen
Remind of former days and ways I ween.
True, the same hills stand on their lasting base,
And like silvery waters flow apace.
All else how changed, with little to denote
How looked this region in the days remote.
Where once the tangled wood extensive spread
We find the fruitful orchard in its stead.
The hunting ground long since was made to yield
To flowery yard and cultivated field.
The costly mansion and the cottage neat,
Which in due order line each pleasant street,
The stores and shops around the busy mart,
Churches and schools adorned by works of art,
Succeed the smoky wigwam frail and low,
A simple shelter from the rain and snow.
By spotted trees o'er tedious trail and drear,
The natives moved, of lurking foes in fear.
In open space, and safely on we press
By rapid cars or the more staid express.
They posted news by the swift runner's speed,
We chain our message to a lightning steed,
And *might* a confab hold with king or queen
While surging ocean rolls between.
Thus great the outward contrast brought to view
As we impressions of the past renew.
In short, they plodded on as in a dream,
We, wide awake, rush through the world by steam.
Nor are the vast improvements of our day,
Attracting notice by their wide display,
Confined to things alone of earthly kind,
But have to do with training of the mind,
With plans for doing good, and scattering light
Through all the different realms of moral night,

Gathering recruits for Zion's holy war,
Sending the gospel to the nations far.
Truly we live in an eventful age,
Calling aloud that each with zeal engage
In leading men in paths of peace and love,
And make this world resemble that above,
While to invite to labor, faith and prayer,
"Signs of the times" in cheering forms declare
The dawning of the morn o'er all the land,
The promise sure, the *victory near at hand.*
So marvel not that no regret we show,
*We* did not live a *hundred* years ago.

Rev. Daniel Dana Tappan of Topsfield, Mass., could not come, so he sent for his part the following, which was read:

GREETINGS TO THIS INTERESTED ASSEMBLAGE OF OLD-TIME FRIENDS AND STRANGERS:

I had no special knowledge of the history of this church previously to my brief residence here; although years before I think I saw the venerable pastor, Rev. Mr. Piper; and later had some acquaintance with Rev. Mr. Barker, having visited at his house, and also officiated at the funeral of his excellent wife. This little speech will refer to matters during my sojourn from Nov. 1865, to June 1871; my ministry closing somewhat earlier. We boarded, the whole time, at Capt. Yeaton's, and had neither cause, nor wish, for a change; not needing, then, and there, the charge given to some early disciples: "*Go not thou from house to house.*" Except at one early period of that ministry, there was no very marked religious interest; nor, at that time, or after, were there known *extensive* happy results of the brief interest. The Sabbath congregations had a fair representation of intelligence, and love of the truth. For a portion of the time, failing to stand, or sit, in their lot, it fell to the preacher, unversed in scientific music, to lead in the service of song, and I fear occasionally missing the right pitch. But the people seemed to take it comfortably, as was but just; as always, when one does as well as he can. It was curious (excuse the remark) that the preacher, who was expected to impart light, was posted aloft, in about the darkest place in the house. And, then, the pulpit was unphilosophically and unsympathisingly high. The minister was thus *set over* the people with a witness:—albeit, some of the brotherhood may be *set under* now. A lawyer would have but a poor prospect of winning a case, himself perched so high, and the jury scattered here and there; not excepting a Choate, or a Webster. Happily, there was no huge sounding-board, threatening the preacher's head, should it become dislodged. But this is past; and you have wisely, and compassionately, brought the minister nearer to the people, to their eyes, and ears, and hearts; for which, on behalf of his successors, and in cordial good will to the congregation, this preacher gives you his felicitations. It was a rather delicate thing to have directly under the eye of the speaker, a cultured, somewhat critical, and very godly, ex-pastor. The relation is a delicate one, usually. But the worthy Mr. Barker decorously listened to his somewhat younger brother; and it is due to say, that once, when the sermon adversely referred to a rather popular usage, on descending from the pulpit he gave the preacher a kind word of approval. Ministers, when called upon to say unpalatable things, need, and may well be grateful for, words of cheer from intelligent, appreciating hearers. I give you this gentle hint gratis. Mr. Barker was ready to assist on Sacramental occasions, and at the Missionary Monthly Concert; and he was almost always present at our social meetings, and ready to help. We had but few, indeed, to take an active part in those meetings, although some true hearted silent ones were, no doubt, in cordial fellowship. The Sabbath evening meetings, usually, at dwelling houses, were cheering and helpful, as some now present may remember; and we used to sing the good old hymns, to the good old tunes, to our hearts' content, as well as we knew how. And, we hope, the Blessed Lord was sometimes with us, in these peaceful gatherings. Our church meetings were almost uniformly desirable. The number admitted to church-membership was very small. Not more than five are now called to mind. But three occasions of baptism are remembered, of adults or infants. One of the infants was a child of Mr. Charles and Mrs. Abby Smith; the other was my grandson, George Francis Dow. On this occasion the baptismal bowl could not seasonably be found,—there not having been an infant baptism for many years. It is hoped that things are better now, if there are any infants to be baptized. We had a happy little meeting, for a while, of young Misses, at Capt. Yeaton's house, spending the time in singing, with perhaps a brief exhortation, and a prayer. The young friends seemed to enjoy it, and it was probably a bond of union between the pastor and those lambs of the flock. Some of those fine girls may be here present to-day, in their maturity, who will recall their kind feelings toward the pastor, and his affectionate wife, now passed to the skies. The church, though few in numbers, had its share of Christly and, of course, lovable members, some of whom have fallen asleep in Jesus, and others have taken, or will take, their places. May they equal, and if they can, through grace, excel those who are now before the throne. In these brief notices, personal references could not well be altogether avoided. But I have tried to escape being overmuch egotistical. An exhortation may not be expected, or fitting, in connection with these reminiscences; but *my best wishes* may be acceptable, for your highest prosperity and usefulness here, and immortal glory hereafter. With respect and best wishes, your friend, DANIEL D. TAPPAN.

Then was sung ,the hymn "Jesus lover of my soul", after which was read the following letter from Rev. George O. Jenness :

CENTRAL CHURCH, ATTLEBORO' FALLS, }
MASS., September 17, 1885. }

Rev. A. H. Thompson, and the Congregational Church at Wakefield, N. H.:

DEAR BRETHREN: I hoped to be present at your Centennial notwithstanding my recent visit among you. But I find it impossible to arrange my affairs here so as to avail myself of the unusual interest and pleasure connected with so important an occasion. My thoughts and good wishes, however, will centre there during the day while you are recounting the many reminiscences connected with the past of the dear old church and parish. While acting pastor there I remember preaching a sort of historical discourse at the time of our country's centennial, taking this text: " Behold, I have graven thee on the palms of my hands, thy walls are continually before me." (Isaiah 49:16.) This promise still remains addressed to all of God's little church households, and while I recall it now and think of your ranks being decimated by death and removals from year to year, I still am filled with many encouraging anticipations for your future. Naturally enough, at this time, my thoughts also revert to the many interesting and profitable seasons I spent in company of some of those associated with me in my work there. I have vividly before my mind Good Father Barker, and our beloved brother Deacon Piper. Since they have both gone home to their glorious reward I frequently recall the sweetness of the fellowship we "once enjoyed". The former was pleased to take a very fatherly interest in me and mine, and many a word of encouragement received I from his kind lips. He was always at our devotional meetings. At the parsonage, I see him now in the arm chair we never forgot to provide him; near the stove in winter, and always just at the left of the door of entrance into the sitting-room. His words were ever edifying and deeply spiritual, and I always felt, if sickness prevented his presence, as if half my support was gone. Nor was he less helpful in the Sanctuary. No minister ever had a more attentive listener than was he. Notwithstanding his age and infirmities I never discovered the least indication of drowsiness during the sermon. In some churches men sleep in sermon time under the plea of hard work all the week, but Father Barker, whose exploits in manual labor were prodigious for a man of more than fourscore, never once fell asleep under my preaching. Of course I ought to say in this connection that this was all the more remarkable since I know that a great deal of my preaching was calculated to make one drowsy. But, if I were to fill a book I should not exhaust the good things I have it in my heart to say of that dear good Father who was such a help and support to me during all my ministry in Wakefield. Neither have I room enough in this to tell how much I loved and honored that venerated saint, Deacon Piper. Fast declined his strength and gradually ebbed away the vigor of his mental powers during the last of my stay in W. But the beauty and fragrance of his Christian faith and love grew brighter and sweeter unto the end. He used frequently to visit me in the parsonage. Always when he came to town meeting would he call. Much delight have I had in recalling those golden hours. Inspiring were his visions of truth, and the undaunted trust in God displayed under the contemplation of the approaching shadows of his earthly life, put to shame many of my weaknesses and fears. After interviews with him my heart invariably sighed, "let my departing be like his". But I have not time and space to tell of all the blessedness I was permitted to experience from my good fortune in having the firm friendship and support of Dea. Piper. Of other dear ones, I would fain speak did time allow. Of Aunt Lucia Dow, of the two Aunt Wiggins, of Aunt Lucy Chesley, and others who were a blessing and help to me and my work, but now have entered into the blessed "rest which remaineth". And if I should attempt to speak of the dear ones *living* whose friendship I was fortunate enough to secure, time and space would also fail me. No place on this earth will ever be dearer to me than Wakefield, and in all my wanderings, the truth compels me to say, I have never found a spot where, if a minister is what he should be, he is more likely to be loved, appreciated and supported. And now as I close, having in my mind still this glowing promise of Isaiah as yet applicable to you, let me urge you to ever keep the "lights" and "fires" on the hill shining and burning as of yore. Do your part well and God will take care that this promise shall be for you, your children and children's children.

> "All is of God! If He but wave His hand
> The mists collect, the rain falls thick and loud,
> Till with a smile of light on sea and land
> Lo! He looks back from the departing cloud."

Very truly and affectionately yours in Christ,

GEO. O. JENNESS.

Capt. Nathaniel Meserve, an old and respected citizen, and for these many years prominent among the Free Will Baptists of Wakefield, being called upon came forward saying he was born in Ossipee, and in a few but telling words cordially eulogized the native town of his wife and the church of her parents, in which she received infant baptism. He paid a warm tribute to a Christian wife and a Christian home. Rev. Charles Dame of Acton, Me., was next called upon and gave the following :

Mr. President: It gives me pleasure to be present on this occasion. It is true I am not a native of Wakefield, but the days of my childhood were passed in sight of some portions of your goodly town. In those days Wakefield was regarded as a vastly important place by the inhabitants of Acton where I then lived. The merits of your physicians were not infrequently discussed, the talents of your lawyers were looked upon with wonder, your merchants were noted for their qualities as men of business. But the man held in the highest esteem, who was the most venerated, whose name was never mentioned but with reverence, was Parson Piper. Comparatively few knew him personally and yet his name is still reverently held by the descendants of that few and many others. But that which more than all things else drew my attention and excited my interest in my youthful days was Dow's Academy, in sight of which many a day was passed. As from the field of labor I looked across the "great East Pond" I gazed upon the academy building and did it with longing eyes that I might enjoy the privileges afforded by this Academy. The sight of this building's tin covered belfry excited desires which nought but a lack of means could suppress. Long will the memory of Dow's famed Academy be cherished by me, permitted as I was to gaze upon it but denied its privileges. It was an honor to Wakefield, an honor to its founder and a blessing to many. Another event which has been a blessing to the town of Wakefield is the long continued residence, the example and influence of Parson Barker. I became acquainted with this godly man about the time of my leaving college. A year or two after graduating and while a member of the Andover Theological Seminary I was spending one of the Seminary's vacations in teaching at Milton Mills and at the same time conducting the Sabbath service for the church at Acton. Not having been ordained to the work of the ministry, or even licensed to preach, I could not administer the ordinances of the church, and as the church at Acton wished to have the sacraments of the Lord's Supper administered to them, I ventured to come to Wakefield and ask the good man if he would go over to Acton and administer the sacrament. Awe struck in his presence and with his tall and venerable form towering above me, I waited for his reply. The reply came from the exact and conscientious man in the form of an objection to my proposal. "You know", he said, "it is against the rules of the Seminary for a student to preach without a license, and I would not wish to do anything that would cast disrespect upon that institution or to encourage any irregularity." The good man after a few explanations and with some hesitation consented to waive his objections and admit the young man into his pulpit. I came with much fear and trepidation to preach in the pulpit of such an one so strong in the faith and so able a man. But as the day proved to be a very rainy one and consequently the audience very small, I saw there was but little chance for the preaching or exhortation of an unlicensed student to do great harm, and probably the Wakefield church passed the day uninjured. But the conscientious scruples of the good man showed his firm regard for law and true and right principles.

Then came the following letter of "Regrets" from one of the former lawyers of Wakefield, Charles Chesley, Esq., which struck a vein of musing that fitted well into the occasion and the closing hour :

WASHINGTON, D. C. <br>September 12, 1885.

Rev. A. H. THOMPSON.

DEAR SIR: I have received your letter of the 9th instant, by which I am informed that, on the 22nd instant, the people propose to observe the one hundredth anniversary of the Organization of the First Church in Wakefield by a Council called by the Town. You express a wish to see me and my family there at that time, and inquire if it would not be agreeable to me to furnish something in writing for the occasion, if I cannot be present ; something, for instance, concerning the schools or the lawyers of Wakefield. It would afford me and my family unbounded pleasure to be present on the occasion named. Wakefield is the "Sweet Auburn" to which "my heart, untravelled, fondly turns." It was there I spent my earliest and happiest days, and there I expect to sleep at last. Memories of a careless boyhood and of early manhood ; memories of the old academy-room, with the mellow autumn sunlight streaming through its broad southern windows upon busy pupils, all happy and free from care like myself; memories of the church, wherein I listened, not too attentively, to words of instruction and advice, both sincere and sound ; memories of the choir,

of which I myself was an inglorious member, and of its weekly
meetings, with the sweet harmony of simple music and the sweeter
harmony of social intercourse; memories of the rugged hills, the
fertile valleys, the noisy brooks, the crystal ponds and the low rus-
tle of waving corn heavy with dew; memories of the sacred grounds
where lie so many of those dearest; these, and a thousand other ten-
der memories arise, even now as I write, and the scenes and asso-
ciations of my young days come back to me, like the sweet strains
of some half-forgotten melody.

But duties, official and unofficial, require my presence here; and
their pressure upon me will prevent my writing anything you
would wish to read or that I should be willing to have read; for,
on such an occasion, one should, ordinarily, give his best or nothing. I thank you for thinking of me and mine in this connection;
but, for the reason already assigned, I can send nothing to your
centennial meeting but our kind remembrances and best wishes.

Faithfully yours,

CHARLES CHESLEY.

In a like vein Rev. A. H. Thompson continued and also
gave the farewell words:

Thus, as we sit at this twilight hour in the dimly lighted
sanctuary with the memories of those olden days crowding
in upon us, we are living in the past. Soon we shall be called back to the present; and in its duties find our chief delight—with joyous hope of the future because of the guiding hand of Him who has guided this church this hundred
years. We shall not sit long by the ashes of the gone out
fire. The light of this day is waning. The twilight deep-
ens. May the day of our life be full of light; and when its
eventide shall come and the night of death, may it be followed by that day without end,—of brightness and of joy—
in the Church of the redeemed in Heaven.

The people arose and joined their voices in the song of
"Auld Lang Syne"; then received the benediction from the
lips of the Pastor, and the SECOND Century was begun.

www.ingramcontent.com/pod-product-compliance
Lightning Source LLC
Chambersburg PA
CBHW021528090426
42739CB00007B/839